AFFILIATE MARKETING FOR BEGINNERS 2020

INTENSIVE COURSE FOR BEGINNERS TO LEARN ABOUT AFFILIATE MARKETING. LEARN IN 30 DAYS HOW TO CREATE YOUR FIRST PASSIVE INCOME WITH THIS FANTASTIC BUSINESS!

BY

RICHARD FLAGG

© Copyright 2020 - Richard Flagg - All rights reserved.

The content contained within this book may not be reproduced, duplicated or transmitted without direct written permission from the author or the publisher.

Under no circumstances will any blame or legal responsibility be held against the publisher, or author, for any damages, reparation, or monetary loss due to the information contained within this book. Either directly or indirectly.

Legal Notice:

This book is copyright protected. This book is only for personal use. You cannot amend, distribute, sell, use, quote or paraphrase any part, or the content within this book, without the consent of the author or publisher.

Disclaimer Notice:

Please note the information contained within this document is for educational and entertainment purposes only. All effort has been executed to present accurate, up to date, and reliable, complete information. No warranties of any kind are declared or implied. Readers acknowledge that the author is not engaging in the rendering of legal, financial, medical or professional advice. The content within this book has been derived from various sources. Please consult a licensed professional before attempting any techniques outlined in this book.

By reading this document, the reader agrees that under no circumstances is the author responsible for any losses, direct or indirect, which are incurred as a result of the use of information contained within this document, including, but not limited to, — errors, omissions, or inaccuracies.

Table of Contents

CHAPTER ONE 7
INTRODUCTION 7
.... 7
    How Affiliate Marketing Can Benefit You............................ 11
    Beginning with Affiliate Marketing 13
CHAPTER TWO 21
THE BASICS OF AFFILIATE MARKETING............................ 21
.... 21
    How Do Affiliate Marketers Get Paid? 24
    Why Be an Affiliate Marketer? 26
    Normal Types of Affiliate Marketing Channels.................. 29
    Tips To Be A Successful Affiliate Marketer........................ 31
    The Top Affiliate Marketing Trends of 2020....................... 34
    Affiliate Marketing for Every Beginners 38
    A Few Last Affiliate Marketing Tips 42
CHAPTER THREE 45
ONLINE WORK TOOLS 45
.... 45
    Product analyst on YouTube.. 53
    Finding on the web take a shot at consultant stages 58
    Web or Graphic creator 59
    Expert, consultant or mentor 62
CHAPTER FOUR.. 66
THE MINDSET TO BE SUCCESSFUL...................................... 66
.... 66
    The Success Mindset: Top 3 Aspects 68

Fruitful Affiliate Marketing 72

The most effective method to switch your mindset and become increasingly fruitful 74

How to Develop Mindset For Success 78

Ways to Develop Your Mindset for Success 82

The Six Pillars of a Successful Mindset for Entrepreneurs 87

The main concern 94

CHAPTER FIVE 96

HOW TO FIND THE WINNING PRODUCT 96

.... 96

Creating an Irresistible Product That Sells Like Crazy 99

Ways to Find Winning Products Every Time 101

How to discover winning products to sell on Shopify? 110

CHAPTER SIX 114

WHICH MARKETING CHANNELS TO USE 114

.... 114

Kinds of Marketing Channels 115

Six Marketing Channels You Can Prioritize in 2020 118

CHAPTER SEVEN 122

HOW MUCH MONEY IT TAKES TO GET STARTED 122

.... 122

So How Much Money Do You Need To Start With Either Of Them? 129

Looking At Starting With Organic Traffic 133

Outline For Free (Organic) Traffic 137

The amount of Money Do You Need To Start Affiliate Marketing. 139

Complimentary gifts You Can Use to Start Affiliate Marketing. ... 143

CHAPTER EIGHT 146

PRACTICAL EXAMPLE 146
.... 146
    The Home Depot And The 'Buyer Search' Site.................................. 148
    What Are The Best Affiliate Programs For Ecommerce? 149
    Affiliate Marketing – Practical Examples Helps To Grow Brands 151
CHAPTER NINE 159
EARNING WITH AFFILIATE MARKETING.................................... 159
.... 159
    The Reality of Affiliate Marketing... 160
    Adjusting Expectations to Earning Potential 163
    The 'Affiliate Marketing" Learning Curve.. 166
CONCLUSION 179
.... 179

CHAPTER ONE

INTRODUCTION

Affiliate marketing is the point at which an online retailer pays you a commission for traffic or deals produced from your referrals. Affiliate marketing is a kind of performance-based marketing in which a business rewards at least one affiliate for every guest or client brought by the affiliate's marketing endeavors. Affiliate marketing covers with other Internet marketing strategies somewhat because members frequently utilize standard promoting techniques. Those techniques incorporate paid search engine marketing, search engine optimization, email marketing, content marketing, and (in some sense) show promoting. Then again, affiliates here and there utilize less universal procedures, for example, distributing audits of products or administrations offered by an accomplice.

Affiliate marketing is usually mistaken for referral marketing, as the two types of marketing utilize outsiders to drive deals to the retailer. The two types of marketing are separated, be that as it may, by the way, they drive sales, where affiliate marketing depends absolutely on monetary inspirations. In contrast, referral marketing depends more on trust and personal connections. Promoters often neglect affiliate marketing. While search engines, email, and site syndication catch a significant part of the consideration of online retailers, affiliate marketing conveys a much lower profile. Affiliates keep on assuming a critical job in e-retailers' marketing procedures.

Affiliate marketing helps to adapt your substance by advancing other organizations' products utilizing affiliate joins. At the point when someone purchases a product or administration dependent on your referral, you win a little commission on that buy. Right now, acquaint you with the rudiments of affiliate marketing and talk about how it functions by and by. We'll likewise give you how you could profit by utilizing it and give you some assistance in the beginning. How about we start! Adapting your website doesn't need to be a troublesome or bargaining try. It very well may be staggeringly fulfilling, both from a financial and imaginative perspective. Also, it does not require much of the legwork associated with different strategies for bringing in cash on the web.

Affiliate marketing includes advancing products from outer sellers on your website. While definitions once in a while change, there are commonly three or four gatherings associated with an affiliate arrangement. Since these terms can be confounding, how about we pause for a minute to explain the 'who' of affiliate marketing:

• The affiliate. Otherwise called 'the marketer,' this is the person running a site that contains affiliate joins. The member gets a commission on each buy made by guests who found a product by clicking on one of their connections.

• The customer. This is a guest on the affiliate site, who clicks on an affiliate interface and finishes a buy (regardless of whether that is the first thing being advanced, or something different from a similar organization).

• The network. This alludes to the inside or outsider stage that the affiliate program is operated on. This means they are giving the connections that the affiliates use and paying the member their bonuses.

- The shipper. This is an organization that sells products being advertised by the affiliate. By and large, the dealer and the network are the equivalents, as individual organizations run their affiliate programs. For straightforwardness, we'll be joining these last two substances all through the remainder of our conversation here.

If that despite everything sounds somewhat befuddling, we should take a gander at a run of the genuine mill case of how an affiliate deal may function:

1. An affiliate shares a blog entry on websites. The post maybe that of a survey of a couple of shoes sold by a dealer.

2. At the base of the post, the affiliate incorporates a connection that prompts the tennis shoes' product page.

3. A buyer peruses the blog entry and, charmed by the audit, clicks on the affiliate connect.

4. Once on the vendor's website, the buyer chooses to buy tennis shoes.

5. The vendor procures a benefit off of the deal and offers a segment of that cash with the affiliate.

You may be interested in how the dealer realizes which affiliate is liable for the buy. That is the simple part as each member is given a special connection that tracks every product they advance. This lets the trader track all referrals and guarantees that they realize how a lot of cash they've earned gratitude to each affiliate and what to pay them consequently.

How Affiliate Marketing Can Benefit You

The possibility to acquire cash by mostly sharing connections most likely sounds enticing as of now. Affiliate marketing incorporates an entire host of favorable circumstances past the conspicuous one. Let's investigate a portion of the ways being an affiliate marketer can profit you and your site.

Above all else, it's a generally safe and reasonable business. The absolute minimum for beginning as an affiliate is having a blog, a website, or even only an online life profile. This makes it an efficient strategy for acquiring cash. It likewise implies you don't need to submit a great deal of money in advance since you can begin little and develop your marketing endeavors after some time.

Another exciting portion of affiliate marketing is that it leaves you alone inventive and give something precious to your crowd. Since you can utilize affiliate connects anyplace, you can set up an audit site, distribute long-structure articles, or even produce video content. Since you're advancing other organizations' products, you don't have to stress over making, delivering, and supporting the things yourself.

Affiliate marketing additionally allows you to pick what you advance. It will also offer you the advantage of being critical. If you get to choose definitely which projects to work with, however much of the time, you'll even select the individual products and administrations you need to advance. You generally have full authority over what's highlighted on the website.

Affiliate marketing can be worthwhile (you, although remember that it is anything but an easy money scam). Since you're acquiring a percentage of each deal you allude, there's no most extreme roof for income either. This implies if your affiliate site takes off in a significant manner, you might wind up making an extraordinary easy revenue.

Considering the entirety of that, you ought to have a genuinely clear thought regarding whether affiliate marketing is something you'd prefer to engage with. For some individuals, the advantages represent themselves. Before you begin posting affiliate joins, there are various things you'll have to tolerate as a primary concern.

How Does Affiliate Marketing Work?

Affiliate marketing is a straightforward 3-advance procedure:

1. You prescribe a product or administration to your devotees.

2. Your devotees buy the product or administration utilizing your affiliate interface.

3. You get paid a commission for the deals made utilizing your affiliate interface.

Beginning with Affiliate Marketing

Presently you know the essential meaning of affiliate marketing and how the procedure functions, so how about we talk about how to begin. Many would-be affiliate marketers don't set aside the effort to design and instead pursue each affiliate marketing network or affiliate marketing program they can discover.

They end up overpowered and over-burden.

Try not to resemble them.

Take as much time as necessary and work through these seven stages if you need to set yourself up for progress.

Complete the initial four stages before you even consider advancing a single product.

1. Discover Your Niche

Do you say "nitch" or "needs?"

Whichever way you say it, choosing a niche will give concentration to businesses and help with the content. It will also make it easier to make focus on marketing efforts.

For specific individuals, picking their niche is the hardest piece of going into business, yet it doesn't need to be that way. To choose your niche, it just takes posing a couple of inquiries:

• What am I enthusiastic about? Ordinarily, the things we're energetic about are things we're likewise definitely learned about, which makes it a lot simpler to create content.

• Is this point sufficiently large? Is there enough to the subject to make up to 100 blog entries? If not, you may battle with search engine optimization or experience difficulty creating authority.

• Is the niche oversaturated? Is there space for another affiliate in the niche? Before hopping into an excessively popular niche and attempting to contend with people who've been around for some time, perhaps check out another slot.

• Is there cash right now? Money isn't all that matters, indeed. In case you're keen on a few points, and one is a money-maker. However, one isn't... pick the money-maker.

You can look at a niche on an affiliate retailer like ClickBank to check whether it merits investing energy into it.

What you're searching for is products that have a high Gravity score, better than average standard pay per deal, and that would fit in generally with your substance. In case you're discovering a lot of products you would have the option to expound on, you've found a profitable niche!

2. Design a Website

When you've found out the right niche that you're ready for, you're prepared to fabricate a website and blog. WP-Beginner has an incredible manual to assist you with picking the best blogging stage that will make this procedure significantly simpler.

The essential focal point of your webpage will be your blog. However, there are a few pages that you ought to consider including (and some that are a level out MUST for affiliate marketers):

1. About: Make it personable and let individuals find a workable pace a bit.

2. Contact: This ought to incorporate all contact data that you need to impart to your perusers, publicists, or potential accomplices.

3. Disclaimer: If your site is adapted, this is the place you share its how.

4. Privacy Policy: Let clients know whether you gather any data about them and how that data is utilized.

5. Terms of Service: This is a legitimate page restricting your risk in case of abuse of data or administrations gave on your site. It additionally subtleties client duties in regards to copyrights and trademarks.

6. Custom 404 Page: A custom 404 page goes far toward improving the client experience.

7. Advertise: If you plan on selling nearby promotions, incorporate a page for publicists with data about accessible spots, month to month sees, crowd socioeconomics, and a contact structure. It's critical to ensure that your arrangements are clear

and forthright to maintain a strategic distance from disarray and to assemble trust with your crowd.

3. Make Quality Content

Since the system of your page is all set, you have to make content.

Some affiliate networks and affiliate programs expect you to as of now have set up content, site traffic, and month to month sees at a specific level before they'll acknowledge you as an affiliate, so make sure to peruse the qualification prerequisites for the particular networks and projects you're thinking about before you apply.

This doesn't imply that you need to make 100 blog entries before you can even consider turning into an affiliate marketer. Yet, you ought to have in any event 5 in number posts as of now on your webpage with progressively booked.

4. Develop Your Email List

Indeed, email is as yet the #1 correspondence channel for marketing. It, despite everything, conveys a wild $38 return for each $1 spent.

Am I not catching this' meaning to you? That it's 3800% justified, despite all the trouble to put some time and cash into developing your email list.

Probably the most effortless approaches to develop your email list is by adding a popup to your site:

Try not to stress if you've never done email marketing; we've all found a good pace. We have a tenderfoot's manual for email marketing that will take you from zero to computerizing your email marketing effort in the blink of an eye.

In case you're hoping to step up your email marketing efforts, look at these posts on diminishing you're withdraw rates and portioning your email list like a genius.

5. Pick Affiliate Products to Promote

If you've accomplished the work to pick a niche, picking affiliate products to advance ought to be simple! Pick products that fit your niche and identify with your substance.

Where do you get thoughts for products to advance? Anyplace, truly:

Advance Products you Already Use

What do you, as of now, use and love? There's most likely an affiliate program for that.

Make a rundown of the entirety of the products and administrations that you use and hit up Google to discover their affiliate programs. At that point, compose surveys and plug in the affiliate joins.

6. Join an Affiliate Marketing Network

Affiliate marketing networks are online commercial centers where retailers list their products, and affiliates can discover products to sell. The marketing network goes about as a go-between. As the affiliate, you ought to never need to pay to pursue an affiliate marketing network.

Here are a couple of the more popular affiliate networks out there, yet there are such a large number of more than this:

- ShareASale

- CJ Affiliate

- ClickBank

- Amazon Associates

This WordPress module lets you dispatch a completely working affiliate program from beginning to end in only a couple of moments. You'll have the option to effectively follow outbound connections, clicks, payments, and deals from your simple to-utilize dashboard, personalized to incorporate just the information that is critical to your objectives.

7. Track Your Results

You can utilize MonsterInsights to handily follow the performance of your affiliate products on a WordPress site.

To begin, you'll have to introduce and enact the MonsterInsights module. At that point, interface your WordPress site with your Google Analytics account.

When actuated, you'll go to Insights » Settings in your WordPress dashboard and select the Tracking tab. s

There are a few segments to the tab. We begin in the Engagement area where you can see that Enable MonsterInsights occasions following defaults to Yes, which is the thing that we need.

CHAPTER TWO

THE BASICS OF AFFILIATE MARKETING

Affiliate marketing is the procedure by which an affiliate gains a commission for marketing someone else's or organization's products. The affiliate essentially searches for a product they appreciate, at that point, advances that product and acquires a bit of the benefit from every deal they make. The arrangements are followed using affiliate joins starting with one website then onto the next.

Since affiliate marketing works by spreading the duties of product marketing and creation across parties, it figures out how to use the capacities of an assortment of people for an increasingly successful marketing technique while furnishing benefactors with a portion of the benefit. To make this work, three unique gatherings must be included:

1. Seller and product makers.

2. The affiliate or publicist.

3. The purchaser.

We should dive into the intricate relationship these three gatherings offer to guarantee affiliate marketing is a triumph.

1. Vender and product makers.

The vender, regardless of whether an independent business person or enormous endeavor, is a seller, dealer, product maker, or retailer with a product to showcase. The product can be a physical article, similar to family unit merchandise or assistance, similar to cosmetics instructional exercises. Otherwise called the brand, the merchant shouldn't be effectively engaged with the marketing. However, they may likewise be the publicist and benefit from the income sharing related to affiliate marketing.

2. The affiliate or distributer.

Otherwise called a distributer, the affiliate can be either an individual or an organization that engagingly advertises the merchant's product to potential buyers. As such, the affiliate elevates the product to persuade buyers that it is significant or useful to them and persuade them to buy the product. If the purchaser ends up purchasing the product, the affiliate gets a bit of the income made.

Affiliates regularly have quite a certain crowd to whom they advertise, for the most part sticking to that crowd's advantages. This makes a characterized niche or personal brand that enables the affiliate to draw in purchasers who will be well on the way to follow up on the advancement.

3. The shopper.

Regardless of whether the shopper knows it or not, they (and their buys) are the drivers of affiliate marketing. Affiliates share these products with them via web-based networking media, web journals, and websites.

At the point when customers purchase the product, the vendor and the affiliate share the benefits. Now and then, the affiliate will decide to be forthright with the shopper by revealing that they are getting a commission for the business they make. On different occasions, the shopper might be unmindful of the affiliate marketing framework behind their buy.

In any case, they will once in a while pay more for the product bought through affiliate marketing; a lot of the benefit is remembered for the retail cost. The shopper will finish the buying procedure and get the product as ordinary, unaffected by the affiliate marketing framework in which they are a huge part.

How Do Affiliate Marketers Get Paid?

A fast and economical technique for bringing in cash without the issue of really selling a product, affiliate marketing has an evident attraction for those hoping to build their pay on the web. Be that as it may, how does an affiliate get paid after connecting the dealer to the shopper? The appropriate response is muddled. The buyer doesn't generally need to purchase the product for the affiliate to get a payoff. Contingent upon the program, the affiliate's commitment to the dealer's deals will be estimated quickly. The affiliate may get paid in different manners:

1. Pay per deal.

This is the standard affiliate marketing structure. Right now, the shipper pays the affiliate a percentage of the deal cost of the product after the purchaser buys the product because of the affiliate's marketing procedures. As such, the affiliate should get the speculator to put resources into the product before they are redressed.

2. Pay per lead.

An increasingly mind-boggling framework, pay per lead affiliate programs, repays the affiliate dependent on the change of leads. The affiliate must persuade the purchaser to visit the shipper's website and complete the ideal activity — regardless of whether it's rounding out a contact structure, pursuing a preliminary of a product, buying into a bulletin, or downloading programming or documents.

3. Pay per click.

This program centers on boosting the affiliate to divert customers from their marketing stage to the trader's website. This implies the affiliate must connect with the buyer to the degree that they will move from the affiliate's site to the vendor's site. The affiliate is paid dependent on the expansion in web traffic.

Why Be an Affiliate Marketer?

What are the motivations to turn into an affiliate marketer?

1. Easy revenue.

While any "ordinary" work expects you to be grinding away to bring in cash, affiliate marketing offers you the capacity to bring in cash while you rest. By putting an underlying measure of time into a crusade, you will consider consistent with being at that time as customers buy the product over the next days and weeks. You get cash for your work long after you've completed it. In any event, when you're not before your PC, your marketing abilities will gain you a consistent progression of salary.

2. No client care.

Singular merchants and organizations offering products or administrations need to manage their shoppers and guarantee they are happy with what they have bought. On account of the affiliate marketing structure, you'll never be worried about client service or consumer loyalty. The total employment of the affiliate marketer is to connect the merchant with the purchaser. The dealer manages any buyer objections after you get your bonus from the deal.

3. Work from home.

In case you're somebody who detests heading off to the workplace, affiliate marketing is the perfect arrangement. You'll have the option to dispatch crusades and get income from the products that dealers make while working from the solace of your own home. This is a vocation you can manage while never escaping your night robe.

4. Financially savvy.

Most businesses require startup charges just as an income to fund the products being sold. Be that as it may, affiliate marketing should be possible effortlessly, which means you can begin rapidly and absent a lot of issues. There are no affiliate program charges to stress over and no compelling reason to make a product. Starting this profession is generally clear.

5. Helpful and adaptable.

Since you're turning into a specialist, you get ultimate freedom in defining your objectives, diverting your way when you feel so slanted, picking the products that intrigue you, and in any event, deciding your hours. This comfort implies you can enhance your portfolio if you like or spotlight exclusively on primary and direct battles. You'll likewise be liberated from organization limitations and guidelines just as sick performing groups.

6. Performance-Based prizes.

With different occupations, you could work an 80-hour week and still acquire a similar compensation. Affiliate marketing is simply founded on your performance. You will get back what you put into it. Sharpening you're looking into abilities and composing drawing in battles will mean direct enhancements in your income. You'll at long last get paid for the extraordinary work you do!

7. Try not to underestimate the power of SEO.

There's a huge amount of natural traffic you can get from search engines if you do SEO properly. The days when Search Engine Optimization was tied in with duping Google are no more. Today, it is tied in with improving your website for guests. Individuals normally search for data on the web. That is the reason you ought to become familiar with the nuts and bolts of on-page SEO, catchphrase research, and third party referencing to be the data source they discover first. Who wouldn't have any desire to rank #1 for terms, for example, "best product" or "product survey" in Google?

Normal Types of Affiliate Marketing Channels

Most affiliates share regular practices to guarantee that their crowd is locked in and open to buying advanced products. In any case, not all affiliates publicize the products similarly. There are a few diverse marketing channels they may use.

1. Influencers.

An influencer is a person who holds the ability to affect the buying choices of a huge fragment of the populace. This person is in an extraordinary situation to profit from affiliate marketing. They, as of now, gloating an amazing after, so it's simple for them to guide buyers to the dealer's products through web-based life posts, websites, and different collaborations with their supporters. The influencers, at that point, get a portion of the benefits they assisted with making.

2. Bloggers.

With the capacity to rank naturally in search engine questions, bloggers exceed expectations at expanding a dealer's changes. The blogger tests the product or administration and afterward composes an extensive survey that convincingly advances the brand, driving traffic back to the vender's website.

The blogger is granted for their impact getting the message out about the estimation of the product, assisting with improving the merchant's deals. For instance, my article on the best email marketing administrations incorporates product surveys, and affiliate connects all through.

3. Paid search centered microsites.

Creating and adapting microsites can likewise collect a genuine measure of deals. These destinations are promoted inside an accomplice site or on the supported postings of a search engine. They are particular and separate from the association's principal site. By offering progressively engaged, important substance to a particular crowd, microsites leads to expanded changes because of their basic and direct source of inspiration.

4. Email records.

Despite its more seasoned starting points, email marketing is as yet a reasonable wellspring of affiliate marketing pay. A few affiliates have email records they can use to advance the vender's products. Others may use email bulletins that incorporate hyperlinks to products, procuring a commission after the buyer buys the product. Another technique is for the affiliate to manufacture an email list after some time. They utilize their different crusades to gather messages as the once huge mob; at that point, convey messages concerning the products they are advancing.

5. Enormous media websites.

They are intended to make a tremendous measure of traffic consistently; these destinations center around building a group of people of millions. These websites elevate products to their large crowd using standards, and relevant affiliate joins. This strategy offers superior presentation and improves transformation rates, bringing about a first-class income for both the vendor and the affiliate.

Tips To Be A Successful Affiliate Marketer

1. Build up compatibility.

When starting your affiliate marketing vocation, you'll need to develop a group of people that has quite certain premiums. This permits you to tailor your affiliate crusades to that niche, improving the probability that you'll change over. By building up yourself as an expert in one zone as opposed to advancing an enormous exhibit of products, you'll have the option to market to the individuals destined to purchase the product.

2. Make it personal.

There is no lack of products you'll have the option to advance. You will be able to see the varieties of products that you put stock in, so ensure that your battles based on really significant products that buyers will appreciate. You'll accomplish an amazing change rate while at the same time building up the unwavering quality of your image.

You'll likewise need to get great at email effort to work with different bloggers and influencers. Utilize a device like ContactOut or Voila Norbert to assemble individuals' contact data and send personalized messages to accumulate visitor blogging and affiliate openings.

3. Begin evaluating products and administrations.

Concentrate on evaluating products and administrations that fall inside your niche. At that point, utilizing the compatibility, you have made with your crowd and your position as an expert, explain to your perusers why they would profit by buying the product or administration you are advancing. Nearly anything sold online can be assessed if there is an affiliate program. In essence, you can survey physical products, computerized programming, or even administrations booked on the web, similar to ride-sharing or travel resort booking. It is particularly powerful to contrast this product with others in a similar classification. Above all, ensure you are producing point by point, articulate substance to improve changes.

4. Utilize a few sources.

Rather than concentrating on only an email crusade, additionally invest energy bringing in cash with a blog, contacting your crowd via web-based networking media, and in any event, investigating cross-channel advancements. Test an assortment of marketing techniques to see which one your crowd reacts to the most. Utilize this system. For more data, you can look at this article on the most proficient method to begin an effective blog this year.

5. Pick crusades with care.

Regardless of how great your marketing abilities are, you'll get less cash-flow on a terrible product than you will on an important one. Set aside the effort to read the interest for a product before advancing it. Try to research the vendor with care before collaborating. Your time is worth very much, and you need to be certain you're spending it on a gainful product and a merchant you can have faith in.

6. Remain current with patterns.

There is not kidding rivalry in the affiliate marketing circle. You'll need to ensure you keep steady over any new patterns to guarantee you stay serious. Moreover, you'll likely have the option to profit by, in any event, a couple of the new marketing methods that are continually being made. Be certain you're staying up with the latest on all these new systems to ensure that your change rates, and in this way income, will be as high as could reasonably be expected.

The Top Affiliate Marketing Trends of 2020

1. Improved affiliate announcing and attribution.

Lots of affiliate programs operate with last-click attribution, where the affiliate accepting the last click before the deal gets 100% acknowledgment for the change. This is evolving. With affiliate stages giving new attribution models and announcing highlights, you can see a full-pipe, cross-channel perspective on how individual marketing strategies are cooperating. For instance, you may see that a paid social crusade created the principal click, Affiliate X got the second click, and Affiliate Y got the last click. Then, you can strategize your affiliate payments, so Affiliate X gets a percentage of the kudos for the deal, although they didn't get the last click.

2. Influencer niches are turning out to be hyper-focused on.

Before, huge affiliates were the backbone, as catch-all coupons and media destinations offered traffic to hundreds or thousands of publicists. This isn't such a lot of the case any longer. With shoppers utilizing long-tail watchwords and searching for quite certain products and administrations, influencers can use their hyper-centered niche for affiliate marketing achievement. Influencers may not send publicists immense measures of traffic. However, the crowd they do send is believable, directed, and has higher change rates.

3. GDPR is changing how personal information is gathered.

The General Data Protection Regulation (GDPR), which produced results on May 25, 2018, is a lot of guidelines overseeing the utilization of personal information over the EU. This is constraining a few affiliates to acquire client information through select in assent (refreshed security strategies and treat sees), regardless of whether they are not situated in the European Union. This new guideline ought to likewise remind you to follow FTC rules and unmistakably reveal that you get affiliate commissions from your suggestions.

4. Affiliate marketers are getting more astute.

Shippers getting an enormous percentage of their income from the affiliate channel can get dependent on their affiliate accomplices. This can prompt affiliate marketers to utilize their significant status to get higher commissions and better arrangements with their promoters. Regardless of whether it's CPA, CPL, or CPC commission structures, there are a ton of lucrative affiliate projects, and affiliate marketers are in the driver's seat.

Best Affiliate Products for Beginners

As you're getting moving, there are three explicit kinds of products I prescribe beginning to showcase. These are ones that will give you the most obvious opportunity with regards to achievement in developing your business and making commissions at a convenient time.

The most effective method to promote an Affiliate Offer

Alright, presently, the most significant part. At this point, you ought to have a decent feeling of what affiliate marketing is, have a thought of what products you need to elevate, and realize how to get your affiliate joins for them. In any case, if you don't have the foggiest idea how to advance them properly, it doesn't generally make a difference presently, isn't that right? Probably not. Right now, going to take a gander at probably the least demanding and best approaches to advance an affiliate offer.

Affiliate Marketing with Product Reviews

If you've developed a great deal of trust with your crowd, product surveys are an awesome method to create a few deals. This works for every one of the three kinds of products you can advance, and I've personally observed accomplishment with each.

The key to an effective product survey is trustworthiness.

I'd commonly just audit things you like, yet if there are disadvantages or easily overlooked details that trouble you – be forthright about them. A great many people realize that no product is perfect, so if you set desires and are unguarded with them, there's a decent possibility they'll get it at any rate.

Ensure you remember the accompanying things for any product survey:

1. A clear feature highlighting your ideal catchphrase ("product name audit" for example)

2. Clear connections for where to purchase at both the top and base of the page

3. A clear proposal

4. A personal tale about how you utilize the product or why you suggest it

Affiliate Marketing for Every Beginners

As we've just referenced, affiliate marketing has a generally low hindrance to passage. To assist you with beginning rapidly, we're going to walk you through the initial steps for transforming your site into an affiliate marketing achievement.

Stage 1: Choose a Suitable Affiliate Niche

In case you're beginning another affiliate site, you'll have to consider what niche you will work inside. Your site's niche figures out what sort of substance you make, who your intended interest group is, and which sorts of products you will advance.

Normally, it's significant to pick a monetarily suitable niche. This shows that you have to place a subject that enough individuals will be keen on. That may appear to be precarious, yet there are, in reality, a ton of choices you can look over. Performing watchword research is likewise a savvy thought at this stage, to discover what catchphrases are driving the most traffic using search engines.

In any case, this progression isn't just about finding the niche that pays the most. You should focus on a niche that suits you personally for effectiveness. If you, as of now, have some information and enthusiasm for your picked region of the center, you'll be in a situation to make legitimate and drawing in substance to oblige your affiliate joins.

You'll likewise have a superior comprehension of your intended interest group's needs and wants. This is basic since it encourages you to manufacture trust with your guests. If they have an inclination that they can depend on your judgment and proposals, they'll be bound to click on your connections and make buys dependent on your recommendations. Hence, the best niche will have a lot of potential buyers and will be something you can make proficient and dependable substance about.

Stage 2: Find and Sign Up for the Right Affiliate Programs

When you have a niche and site all set, it's an ideal opportunity to search for affiliate programs. As we referenced already, numerous projects are run legitimately by a dealer, to advance their own organization's products.

While selecting which projects to pursue, you should initially take a gander at what products they need you to advance. Above all, they'll have to offer products that are famous in your chosen niche. Subsequently, search for brands that address your objective market and check whether they offer affiliate programs. If your webpage is in with running websites, you could search for the web has with their affiliate programs.

Usually, it's likewise essential to discover programs that will pay you well. All things considered, you're investing a great deal of energy into advancing the traders' products, so you should see a decent amount of the benefits. Before you join, it's likewise a savvy move to research each program and see what experiences different affiliates have had.

You may even think that its helpful to search out an affiliate network, for example, Wealthy Affiliate. There, you can get guidance and help from the individuals who have been distributing and marketing for quite a while. This can be especially useful when you're an amateur. At that point, in a couple of years, you may be the one helping another learner begin.

Stage 3: Add Affiliate Links to Your Site

Now, you've pursued the best affiliate programs in your deliberately picked niche. Presently it's an excellent opportunity to indeed find a workable pace, implies sharing your affiliate joins. How you execute these connections on your site will shift, contingent upon what kind of substance you're making.

For instance, in case you're running a survey site, it bodes well to put principal affiliate connects inside your audits. The easiest method for doing this is simply to incorporate them as content connections in the substance itself. Notwithstanding, this methodology can be viewed as deceiving since it's less confident that you're advancing the products being referred to.

A superior method is to keep your connections somewhat isolated from your fundamental substance.

Some affiliate projects will likewise give you resources, for example, pennants, that you can use to advance products. This may be increasingly appropriate if you need to keep your marketing and substance unmistakably isolated.

Similarly, as with your niche, your way of dealing with actualizing connections will rely upon your site's motivation. Don't hesitate to experiment with various procedures; however, consistently recall that your attention ought to be on offering some benefit to your crowd. If you flop in that task, guests won't trust you, click on your connections, or return later on. Ensure you compose quality substance, in this manner, and watch out for your changes to perceive what's working (and so forth).

At last, we by and by the need to pressure the significance of unveiling your affiliate joins. This is an essential piece of conforming to the support rules given by the FTC. Damaging these rules could prompt lawful activity, which is usually something you'll need to stay away from, no matter what.

Like this, you ought to give data about your connections' tendency and reason, which you can do by making an 'affiliate divulgence' articulation. The notification ought to be unambiguous, and noticeable anyplace affiliate joins are utilized. This will keep your site in the clear, and help to advance trust with your crowd.

A Few Last Affiliate Marketing Tips

If you track with the methodologies above, you'll be making affiliate deals instantly off of your blog.

To improve your odds considerably more, I have a couple more tips for you.

Utilize Pretty Link

Affiliate joins are commonly genuinely revolting. They're long connections that frequently go to an optional area, and are entirely evident that they're an affiliate. Download the Pretty module Link to make your contacts look substantially more benevolent.

Build up a Good Relationship with an Affiliate Manager

Most significant affiliate programs for physical products or administrations will have an affiliate supervisor, whose sole occupation is to assist you with creating more deals.

You'll have to demonstrate to them that you have some potential, however, give a valiant effort to get them on the telephone before you begin doing any significant advancements. They'll have the option to provide you with a decent feeling of what works, what doesn't, and conceivably even give you a lift in commissions. One call about multiplied my payments for one is facilitating organization specifically.

Affiliate Marketing Alternatives: Four Other Online Businesses to Supplement Your Affiliate Marketing Business

• Freelance Writing – The least demanding approach to begin a business on the web, begin constructing a few aptitudes, and building trust in your capacity to effectively accomplish something like affiliate marketing.

• Niche Sites – Once you get the nuts and bolts of affiliate marketing down, you can genuinely focus on rehashing the procedure and making niche destinations on a wide range of various subjects.

• Blogging – A large segment of each excellent affiliate marketing website is the blog, take that range of abilities and make an interpretation of it into another business.

• Physical Products – Want to make a physical product that integrates with your niche and afterward sells it on the web? If you need to work at it, there's a considerable amount of chance here.

CHAPTER THREE

ONLINE WORK TOOLS

There are a vast amount of these apparatuses presented each day; these are only a couple of our top picks:

1. Adblock Plus

AdBlock Plus strips Flash advertisements, pop-ups, and inserted activities on any site you see, including Facebook and YouTube. It additionally squares malware to secure your PC. Accessible for IE, Firefox, Safari, Chrome, and Android OS.

2. Aura

Aura offers note, screen catch, and an image cutting instrument to assist you with recollecting relevant data or motivation found on the web. Their suite of tools permits you to catch and offer substance from locales through an augmentation on different internet browsers. Their cut-out apparatuses provide heaps of adaptability to find different parts or even whole site page scrolls.

3. Blog Social Analyzer

Blog Social Analyzer lets you check your blog or another organization's RSS channel to locate some essential realities, for example, Alexa, MozRank and Domain Authority, and to perceive how a lot of online networking sharing is going on. Use it to assess yourself or to check whether offers are basic on a blog you're considering visitor posting for. This one is an essential online apparatus and doesn't require a module or expansion.

4. Disengage

Disengage prevents destinations from following your developments on the web. It squares outsider treats, gives you command over site contents, and shields your protection from prying "eyes." The free form runs on Chrome, Firefox, and Opera.

The superior rendition is accessible for Mac, PC, iOS, and Android.

5. dotEPUB

Date pub spares online articles and transforms them into epub documents you can open later on an assortment of eReaders or practically any cell phone. Accessible for Chrome and Firefox, additionally as a bookmark on different programs.

6. Evernote web clipper

Evernote web clipper lets you get almost anything on the web and set it back into an Evernote scratchpad. It matches up overall gadgets with your record to review significant web bits. What is particularly extraordinary about this instrument is its capacity to feature critical data and include notes while including the passage. Accessible for IE, Firefox, Safari, Chrome, and Opera.

7. Ghostery

Ghostery is like Disconnect, giving you labels, web bugs, pixels, and reference points that are remembered for pages to follow your online conduct. Ghostery approaches a library of 4,500 contents and screens more than 2,200 trackers, giving you a move call of the promotion networks, conduct information suppliers, web distributers, and different organizations intrigued by your action, letting you deny them from gathering your data. Accessible for IE, Safari, and Opera.

8. Hootlet

Hootlet lets you watch a hashtag (HootFeed in HootSuite) with live updates directly from your program while surfing different pages. You can likewise plan presents on different social stages, including Twitter, LinkedIn, Pinterest, Instagram, YouTube, Google maps, and the sky is the limit from there. Accessible for Firefox and Chrome.

9. HoverZoom

HoverZoom extends thumbnails on mouse-overs to full-estimate pictures. HoverZoom takes a shot at destinations like Facebook, Tumblr, and Amazon for simple amplification and a quicker perusing experience. Accessible for Google Chrome as it were.

10. GIPHY

GIPHY delineates your substance, email message, or blog entry with the perfect energized GIF quickly. It is a search expansion that permits you to type in catchphrases to search, select, at that point intuitive into Gmail, Facebook, Twitter, Slack, Hipchat, and the sky is the limit from there.

11. TooManyTabs

TooManyTabs tidies up your work area by sorting out the tabs you have open. You can sort out bookmarks by creation time, space, or title, see every tab's substance, and reestablish as of late shut tabs. Accessible for Chrome as it were.

12. Grammarly

Grammarly is an augmentation that improves and triple check your internet composing. It surveys spelling, syntax, and even plagiarism. It underlines and proposes remedies almost any place you compose on the web, including Gmail, Facebook, Twitter, Tumblr, and LinkedIn. Accessible for Chrome, Safari, and Firefox.

13. Canva

Canva is a visual communication programming where you can without much of stretch prepare illustrations for web-based life, introductions, and additionally utilizing their pre-stacked formats or by making your own. There are free pictures, vectors, and textual styles to effectively and rapidly make proficient looking designs. Takes a shot at Chrome, Firefox, Safari, Internet Explorer and Microsoft Edge.

14. PlaceIt

PlaceIt is a mockup generator that permits you to put plans or pictures on a mockup without messing around in Photoshop. It has an enormous assortment of photographs and recordings to browse, including clothing and different gadget screens. New pictures are included much of the time by their staff picture takers.

15. Found's SEO Audit Tool

Found's SEO Audit Tool permits you to survey SEO mistakes on your site page in short order. You should simply reorder your space and click a catch. A report will stack that gives blunders, alerts, and triumphs concerning your SEO strategies. You can send out the information into a PDF so you can address the discoveries.

16. MeisterTask

MeisterTask is a venture the board apparatus that permits you to mind map undertakings and see your entire day initially. You can organize projects dependent on which to concentrate on for the afternoon, immediately message colleagues, and even imprint task connections in classifications: identified with, copied, or blocked. This instrument incorporates Google Drive, Dropbox, Slack, and the sky is the limit from there.

You are beginning your online business.

If you have decided to work at home as opposed to having a regular office work, odds are you'll like to work for yourself while accomplishing on the web fill in also. These online employments will let you deal with your own time, understand your latent capacity, and, as a rule, gain significant cash.

Maker (selling your specialty on the web)

If you are capable of any specialties or plan, there is certainly a business opportunity for your craft. Unquestionably, you can sell your manifestations in disconnected occasions like artworks fairs or Christmas markets. Be that as it may, trading on the web will presumably be increasingly gainful and may even transform into full-time online work, mainly if a portion of your specialty is computerized.

Some incredible stages for selling your work on the web:

• Facebook is the brightest spot to start. Make a page for your product or brand, welcome all of your contacts to join and think about a test with free giveaways. Like this, you will get the message out about your product and get your first fan base. You can, in like manner, add a shop to your Facebook page or join Facebook Marketplace that enables buying and selling straightforwardly in the application.

• Etsy is the most acclaimed stage for exhibiting carefully assembled things. Regardless of whether your fine art is advanced, you can sell it here. A few models are wedding greeting layouts, superior banners, diaries, objective organizers, and plans for the day, structure maps, and so on.

• If your craft is less substantial, you can make your online store with Sellfy. Innovative business visionaries utilize this instrument to sell digital products like video or photograph presets, digital books or copywriting formats, liveliness, jingles, beats, or sewing designs.

Sell T-shirts, banners, mugs, caps, or even sacks with your plan or wonderful statements. Outsourcing administrations like Printful handle all the printing, bundling, marking, and in any event, sending in your place. You simply need to transfer plans, draw in purchasers, and afterward get your benefit. A few clients have announced acquiring over $1,200 in three weeks with this administration.

Product analyst on YouTube

The vast majority of us have checked a product survey on YouTube before buying. Can you be on the other side of the screen and offering your product audit recordings? Fortunately, you can audit products in your preferred niche – be it tech, excellence, home stylistic theme, wellness, or some other.

Here are a few different ways to acquire by putting product surveys on YouTube:

• YouTube promotions – if you get a lot of perspectives, publicizing can be a decent wellspring of salary.

• Affiliate marketing – place an affiliate interface in the video portrayal and get a percentage of the deal.

• Get paid to deliver supported surveys – get enlisted by brands to do explicit product audits. Websites like Famebit and Grapevine are a decent spot to search for paid sponsorships.

With time, you can develop your audience, gain impact, and work out more arrangements surveying products that you love.

Affiliate marketer

Affiliate marketing is the way toward helping another website to sell their products or administrations through uncommon affiliate joins. At the point when you pursue an organization's affiliate stage, you'll get your one of a kind connection or connections, that will gain you a commission each time a client clicks on them (or purchases something in the wake of clicking).

Numerous bloggers use affiliate marketing as an online work to gain cash from their composition. You don't need to be an essayist to take in substantial income along these lines – you can advance affiliate connects on your YouTube channel, web-based life, Facebook gatherings or discussions, blog entry remarks, and so forth. The greatest reward of affiliate marketing is that it liberates you from the duties of conventional deals models, such as having a product, website, or deals engine.

Blogger

As portrayed above, affiliate marketing is a boundless wellspring of salary for bloggers. In any case, you can procure cash as an essayist utilizing different ways as well. Some different approaches to win as a blogger (other than affiliate marketing):

• Placing advertisements on your blog and getting paid each time a guest clicks on them.

• They are writing audits about other organizations' products or administrations. Ensure they are significant to your audience and that they are not your solitary substance.

• Offering extra paid substance inside your articles (e.g., downloadable digital book, online meetings, or related products).

• You are doing content marketing for your clients. You can either compose articles for your customer's blog, or pitch visitor presents on respectable stages, including connections to your customer's webpage. Your client will pay you for getting the message out about their administrations and improving their positioning in search engines.

• I am writing for different web journals and news sources that pay visitor supporters.

The huge advantage of blogging is that you needn't bother with any spending limit to begin it – just great composing abilities and expertise in a niche theme or an interesting experience.

Affiliate

Exchanging implies discovering minimal effort in things that you can sell for additional. This can be available online work if you have extraordinary abilities or information that lets you find out products that are less available to others. In this manner, they would be glad to pay more to have these products brought to them by you. For instance, you might be a master in discovering forte things, incredible carport deals, or old pieces. Or then again, you might be a middle person between states or nations – recognizing something modest in one spot and offering it to another audience.

You can even begin by selling the things you have at home and never again need. For exchanges, you can either make your online store or sell stuff on destinations like eBay.

Picture taker

If you love taking photographs, you can rapidly transform this leisure activity into a wellspring of salary. Here are a few different ways picture takers can procure cash on the web:

• Teach photography. Offer valuable hints and procedures that hopeful picture takers couldn't want anything more than to catch wind of.

• Sell banners or advanced work of art. See point No—1 (Selling your specialty on the web).

• Sell your photographs on stock websites. Shutterstock, iStock, and BigStock are the most well-known photograph databases. The amount paid for each download is commonly low, so you should wager on the amount and transfer new groups of photographs consistently. The way to getting saw on stock websites is including numerous important watchwords that individuals would search for.

• Offer your photography and photograph altering aptitudes on specialist stages (see the accompanying area about Finding on the web deal with consultant stages)

Website analyzer

Numerous websites lose cash because of a poor UI, lousy route, and hazy duplicate or terrible structure. Accordingly, organizations search for individuals to test and survey their site before propelling it. Much of the time, you'll have to talk your musings for all to hear and record your screen activities as you peruse the website. For the most part, tests take between 5-25 minutes to finish, and the pay is an average of $10 per test.

Here's a rundown of stages that join website proprietors and analyzers and can offer great online work to do on aside.

Finding on the web take a shot at consultant stages

If you aren't prepared to wander into your own online business, offering your administrations on specialist stages is a decent spot to begin online work. Probably the most well-known specialist stages incorporate Fiverr, Upwork, and Freelancer. Other than joining these stages, there are different approaches to locate your first clients. For instance, using your companions and expert contacts; by sharing your portfolio on your internet based life; or by connecting with organizations straightforwardly (e.g., offering a copywriting administration to a website with an imperfect duplicate).

On the whole, characterize your ability and make it your calling.

Publicist, interpreter or editor

If composing is your quality, you can undoubtedly transform it into a wellspring of pay. You may be underestimating acceptable composition – everybody can write, isn't that so? Numerous individuals are not talented in making deals messages, thorough portrayals, or even internet-based life posts. There's an enormous audience glad to re-appropriate such undertakings.

Additionally, numerous business visionaries compose their website messages or blog articles that simply need altering and editing, or interpretation for different markets. All you have to do to catch that customer base is offer them your abilities and experience. Express your subject matters in your resume and provide instances of your work – along these lines, you'll stand apart from the opposition.

Web or Graphic creator

In our advanced period, visual depiction works are more requested than any other time in recent memory.

If you have some structure aptitudes and experience, these are only a few sorts of online work you can do:

• Website and presentation page structure

• Logo structure

• Mobile application structure

• Business cards and corporate gifts

- Ads, pennants and marketing materials

- Leaflets, pamphlets, digital books

- Packaging structure

- Presentation structure

- Diverse delineations

Other than specialist stages, there are different dependable approaches to bring in some additional cash with your plan work.

Language guide

Individuals have been anxious to learn new dialects since old occasions. Fortunately, it's a lot simpler to ace another dialect today than it was hundreds of years or even decades back. Doesn't make a difference if your native language is English or any of the world's 7000 languages. You make certain to discover understudies ready to learn or rehearse with you.

Far superior if you, as of now, make them instruct experience. If you don't, add a particular component to your resume. For instance, you may remember some social realities for your course, or make your classes' additional enjoyment, casual, or adaptable for any hour of the day – whatever is your thing.

Voice over

Various businesses are searching for male or female voices to portray their marketing or explainer recordings. Moreover, book recordings, web recording introductions, TV/Radio advertisements, instructional exercises, and even phone messages all require proficient voice overs.

If you have astounding vocal aptitudes in your local language, there's an immense open door for you to win cash with them. The best part – this activity is anything but difficult to do as all you need is a PC, a great amplifier, and alive with respectable acoustics.

Client assistance delegate

Numerous organizations are hoping to re-appropriate client care – particularly if their customer base is worldwide and they can't furnish nonstop help with their group. If you are into helping individuals or might want to construct experience right now, your administrations on specialist stages is a decent spot to begin.

Email, web-based life, and talk support just as lead age are the most widely recognized undertakings of a redistributed client assistance delegate. Nonetheless, the more extensive the scope of administrations you offer, the higher your possibility of getting contracted. For instance, you can include information passage occupations, web-based life the executives, report planning, and different obligations to your resume.

On the opposite side, you can function as a riddle shopper assessing the client care nature of other online shops and websites. Psyche that to have this as a genuine online work, you'll have to do a lot of secret shopping.

Expert, consultant or mentor

If you are an expert in truly any region, some individuals need to get your point of view and gain from your experience.

These are only a few instances of various zones you can counsel on:

• Business and Entrepreneurship

• Marketing and deals

• Freelancing

- Relationships

- Health and Fitness

- Fashion and Style

- Parenting

- Interior structure

- Writing

Investigate the classifications on consultant stages and offer your recommendation during the ones pertinent to your calling or experience. For instance, if you have dealt with an independent company, offer your meetings under Business or Marketing classifications.

Bookkeeper

Planning and funds are the bad dreams of numerous business people; no big surprise incalculable businesses are searching for approaches to re-appropriate these perplexing errands. If you are acceptable with numbers and make them account experience to appear, your customer base is without a doubt out there.

Shockingly better if you have lawful information, such as setting up a business, getting ready agreements, or enrolling your trademark. This might be an aptitude applicable in your area, yet at the same time profoundly requested.

Menial helper

The elements of a menial helper can go from straightforward assignments like information passage or interpreting discussions to progressively complex web research and examination, lead age, Photoshop alters, travel arranging, top to bottom LinkedIn search, and bookkeeping.

Start by characterizing your expertise and offering it on one of the consultant locales. The more extensive your range of abilities and the better your audits, the more probable you are to bring home the bacon from this sort of online work. Menial helpers in the United States procure $15.57 per hour.

Web-based life director

This activity is now and again recorded under a menial helper. In any case, as web-based life, the board is a profoundly requested expertise, bosses regularly search for it independently. If you are an authority of web-based life, you can make administration bundles that businesses could purchase from you. Essential online networking the executives' month to month bundle could include:

• Setting up an online networking profile (if vital)

• Monitoring 3-5 online networking stages, by noting remarks and messages

• Creating substance and posting a few times each week

• Adding applicable hashtags, pictures, and connections

Internet-based life the executives is a generously compensated kind of online work that is sought after. It is likewise an entirely adaptable activity as you can plan the posts whenever and anyplace.

If you pick this way, think about working with a few clients simultaneously to boost your pay.

CHAPTER FOUR

THE MINDSET TO BE SUCCESSFUL

In this day and age, having a triumph mindset is significant. It permits you the adaptability to see the various prospects and steps expected to take care of business. Regardless of whether it's in sports, business, the scholarly world, or amusement; Individuals with a triumph mindset consistently appear to make sense of how to get things going, despite apparently unthinkable odds. Some true instances of individuals with a triumph mindset are those with troublesome childhoods who have proceeded to make stunning things out of themselves. We've seen pioneers who've figured out how to battle extraordinary conditions and secure achievement. They've all had a similar shared characteristic, a point of view or conviction framework called the achievement mindset.

In a fixed mindset, individuals accept their fundamental characteristics, similar to their insight or ability, are fixed attributes. They invest their energy recording their knowledge or ability as opposed to creating them. They additionally accept that ability alone makes achievement—without exertion. These kinds of individuals feel crushed after a disappointment and step away from difficulties outside their customary range of familiarity.

In a development mindset, individuals accept that their most fundamental capacities can be created through devotion and challenging work—cerebrums and ability are only the beginning stage. This view makes an adoration for learning and flexibility that is basic for extraordinary achievement. These sorts of individuals see difficulties and disappointments as chances to learn and develop. They persist despite misfortunes. This mindset is a sign of accomplishment and achievement.

We, as a whole, have a few shades of both development and fixed mindsets, contingent upon the circumstance. Developing a development mindset will improve your capacity to prevail in all everyday issues. Learning a development mindset makes inspiration and productivity in the realms of business, instruction, and sports. It influences how you lead, oversee, parent, and appear seeing someone. Consider how you last moved toward a test: with interest for what you could realize or by pondering how you may show up if things turned out badly? If the last mentioned, it may be the ideal opportunity for a mindset change.

The Success Mindset: Top 3 Aspects

We here at Acquirent think three things characterize this achievement mindset:

1. A Growth Mindset

A development mindset is accepting that you can turn out to be better and improve with time and practice. Having a fixed mindset is imagining that there are parts of your personality and range of abilities that can't be enhanced past your current state. One model is knowledge. A development mindset accepts that a person can raise their IQ or information with study and practice. In any case, somebody with a fixed mindset takes that your IQ is the thing that it is. If you are awful at math, it doesn't make a difference in the amount you practice; there are ideas that you will not be able to get a handle on.

2. An Inward-Looking Propensity

N a nutshell, this is simply the capacity to search internally. It is challenging to have a triumph mindset without mindfulness. Ensure you are pointing fingers at yourself in all circumstances, even great ones. Might you be able to have accomplished something other than what's expected that would permit you to improve later on? Some significant inquiries to pose to yourself are:

• What did I gain from the circumstance?

• How am I developing?

• What might I be able to have done?

Asking yourself these inquiries keeps you continually looking forward and pushing ahead.

3. Positive Possibilities

Our third part of having a triumph mindset is accepting positive opportunities for yourself. This isn't visually impaired good faith and doesn't mean you ought to take that you can do everything. For instance, if you are 5'5" and trust you can dominate, that doesn't mean you can do it. In any case, if you can understand the real chance that you can improve your shot, bit by bit, you can grow as a bounce shooter. This is the conviction that positive changes can occur when we find a way to get it going.

It takes practice to embrace a triumph mindset for the individuals who don't as of now have one. If you trust you can change your viewpoint, at that point, you can begin by investigating yourself and making sense of the means you can take to adjust your psyche toward an increasingly fruitful perspective.

In deals, this could begin with defining objectives or tuning in to your calls. You may choose to adjust your contents, follow up additional, or take a shot at your tuning in. Whatever it is, you should begin with trusting it is conceivable to show signs of improvement, at that point, give yourself the time and commitment to improving.

Why it's a higher priority than any time in recent memory to develop your development mindset.

These circumstances are just going to turn out to visit progressively. At no other time has the universe of work been assaulted with such a lot of progress, change from all edges, change that implies that businesses and the individuals that work inside them must adjust, test, learn and challenge themselves on a close to everyday schedule.

For most, this implies operating outside of our customary ranges of familiarity all the more regularly. It means a move from working in set circles where we realize we can perform well, rings in which there's no perceived danger of disappointment or of looking dumb. A transition to managing various divisions and outside accomplices and providers all the more routinely, to cooperating with individuals who we may esteem more educated than us, individuals we are bound to see as a risk.

Thus, to be effective in this day and age of work, and later on, we should all show signs of improvement at thriving in these sorts of testing circumstances, rather than giving the story access our heads dominate. We should improve at persisting with those issues we would have once slowed down finished – surrendering at last. We should enhance at looking for motivation from the individuals we would have once avoided. We should all move our mindset to see the world and everything in it as a ceaseless chance to learn. Since, when we do, we're unmistakably more probable future-evidence our aptitudes and expertise.

Managers perceive this as well, with many trying to pull in contender to their businesses who are unmistakably ready to put time and exertion into building up their capacities, as opposed to the individuals who accept their abilities in specific zones are fixed, never to be extended and improved. These are the individuals who can genuinely assist them in driving their businesses forward.

Things being what they are, how might you move from a fixed to a development mindset, and become progressively employable simultaneously?

Fruitful Affiliate Marketing

It tends to be hard to win a consistent pay from affiliate marketing, and significantly increasingly hard to stand apart among different marketers advancing similar products. When you've developed a website, blog, pamphlet, or online life, there are steps you can take to get useful and create a progressively dependable income stream.

1. Know your accomplices. Research each affiliate program you consider joining with the goal that you will see how and when you'll be paid.

2. Build trust. Purchase the products you plan to advertise so you can personally authenticate the quality. You'll be decided by the product or administration you advance, so center around the nature of your image and suggestions, not merely the winning

potential. Your adherents will come to confide in your proposals and be bound to purchase from you.

3. Have a brand. Pick affiliate things that coordinate your niche and the substance of your blog. Try not to depend on SEO or web-based social networking alone to drive individuals to your website and affiliate referrals. Comprehend who your objective market is, the place you can discover your audience, and how to allure clients on your site.

4. Use assortment. Blend and match affiliate promotions, so you don't overpower your guests (content-inserted affiliate interfaces, as a rule, have the best click-through rates over picture joins.) Consider utilizing a lead page and pipe framework to showcase your affiliate business. Draw possibilities to your email list with a free offer and incorporate connects to your affiliate product pages.

5. Know the lawful prerequisites. Most guests will presumably comprehend that notices lead to your pay. Yet, if you compose a survey or utilize an in-content connection as a suggestion, you should expressly express that each buy utilizing that connection can produce income for you. This isn't merely an acceptable business: it's additionally legally necessary. If you don't unveil affiliate or income-producing joins, you could confront legal and monetary penalties.6

6. Track your traffic and income. Screen the accomplishment of your affiliate programs, primarily if you work with a few unique ones. Realize which projects are the best and which products reverberate with your adherents so you can design future battles.

Like some other sort of home business, achievement in affiliate marketing relies upon contributing the time and exertion to develop your business and manufacture associations with your clients and accomplice brands.

If you choose to seek after affiliate marketing, comprehend that it is anything but a quick or programmed business model. Be that as it may, it is conceivable to gain dependable and legitimate pay as an affiliate marketer.

The most effective method to switch your mindset and become increasingly fruitful

I'm no expert right now, having perused around this subject and thought about my own experience. I believe there are a couple of things you can begin doing today to develop your development mindset and help secure your future profession achievement:

1. Become progressively mindful: Reflect on what your run of the mill reaction is when confronted with specific difficulties, what triggers you to change into a fixed mindset and how might you come back to a place of development? Do you stress over not being 'adequate' or question your capacity to discover an answer for an issue you believe you don't have what it takes to understand? Do you feel overpowered and dread disappointment, so concentrate on different errands, assignments that you know you're generally acceptable at? When given input, do you think your guards go up? What I'm attempting to state here is that you have to think about how you feel at those key 'trigger' minutes, tuning in to the voice in your mind and what it's letting you know. At the point when you do, you'll have the option to choose those unhelpful self-constraining stories going around in your mind, accounts that you'll have to quietness if you are to move from a fixed to a development mindset in any meaningful manner.

2. Comprehend that your mind works like a muscle, it very well may be prepared: This marvel is known as neuroplasticity, as has been clarified by Professor and Neuroscientist Michael Merzenich, the man generally acclaimed as the dad of the idea of cerebrum versatility. Experiments have indicated that not exclusively is the cerebrum intended to change, yet additionally, it's working can be improved at any stage. Merzenich clarifies right now the human cerebrum works a lot of like a muscle,

requiring difficulties to develop. You accordingly can't anticipate that your mind should develop in case you're continually doing things likewise, and not testing it. Instead, Merzenich says that you have to remain in 'challenge mode.' Simply consider the way toward getting fit; it takes reps and practice to manufacture muscle, the cerebrum is the same. To create expertise in a particular territory, comprehend that it's not your cerebrum that is preventing you from doing only that, it's your mindset.

3. Reliably pick testing errands as opposed to safe ones: Overcome your dread of disappointment or looking dumb, disregard any self-question you have, and center your time and vitality around those undertakings you perceive to be more troublesome than others on your plan for the day. At the point when you do, attempt to decipher and handle these from a mindset of development. Honestly, you may fall flat. In any case, all the while, you'll get the hang of something vital to you that you wouldn't have done something else – including what you can do next time to guarantee you improve later on. With a move in mindset and working on receiving this mindset, you can rapidly grow your abilities as you're beginning to move toward each new test with energy and certainty, rather than with evasion and dread.

4. If you think somebody is superior to you, don't consider them to be a risk: Instead, change how you feel to find how you can gain

from them. This person you perceive to be compromising or scaring may have technical expertise that would assist you with leaping forward on one of your activities that have been on stop – or perhaps they simply have a specific method for getting things done, of acquiring answers to an issue that you had never thought of. Begin to move your intuition to understand that everybody you experience is a chance to take in something or understand things from with an improved point of view – that is not something to feel undermined by that is something to grasp.

5. Comprehend that you're not going to ace another ability medium-term: Remember we're never tantamount to us can be at a given aptitude when we begin rehearsing it – rather, it takes work and effort to ace. In this way, at whatever point you take on another test or set out on learning another ability, quit squeezing yourself. Rather, comprehend that you will experience battles toward the start. Pick something that you can't do right now – that one thing that you've generally had an inability to think straight about. Invest energy rehearsing it. Try not to stress over not being accepted at it straight away, or about another person is better. Simply center on your learning venture, beginning little and building your abilities a little bit at a time from that point. After some time, you'll begin to see improvement. In essence, this will fortify your tendency and certainty with regards to getting the hang of, which means you're unmistakably bound to proceed on that venture, as opposed to rescuing at the primary obstacle.

6. Put forth an informed attempt to commit time and exertion (and don't surrender): Just think about all the abilities you could have added to your repertoire, that your fixed mindset is preventing you from creating – those things that could have won you that advancement before or are so significant to developing your organization. Try not to come up with the rationalization that you "need more time," to create them, or "that is another person's activity"– rather, cut out the time. The most elevated accomplishing individuals in history valued this. Simply take a gander at Albert Einstein, who saw that "it isn't so much that I'm so savvy, it's simply that I remain with issues longer."

Along these lines, for your vocation achievement, this is the ideal opportunity to move your perspective, to hinder those harming considerations that hover in your psyche, those contemplations that can deny you of the chance to construct new aptitudes – abilities that could help secure your future employability.

How to Develop Mindset For Success

Achievement isn't a move that you make; it's a lifestyle. If you need to achieve extraordinary things, enormity must be reflected in everything that you do.

Consequently, paying little heed to what it is you need to achieve, the way to progress must start by receiving the correct mindset.

Coming up next are five hints to build up the perfect mindset for progress.

1. Characterize What Success Means

The initial step to building a mindset for progress is to characterize succeeding.

Defining objectives for yourself makes it simpler to think of a strategy to accomplish your aspirations, and will persuade you to make that arrangement. It likewise gives you a standard against which to gauge your advance and change your system. You should consequently characterize life or professional objectives and afterward consider what you have to do to accomplish them. Take a stab at defining SMART Goals in every aspect of your life that you need to change.

What's more, make momentary every day or week, making a point to adjust them to your more extensive positions. In case you're experiencing difficulty figuring out where to begin, look at my Goal's Quickstart Masterclass to assist you with defining and accomplish any objective.

2. Keep in contact With Your Intuition

The second means of building a mindset for progress is to keep in contact with your instinct.

Many accept that achievement implies settling on determined choices dependent on exact information. While you should attempt to be as experimental as could reasonably be expected, such information isn't always accessible. Regardless of your particular way, you will probably need to settle on a choice sooner or later during your life or vocation where there is no measurable answer.

Right now, you must have the option to tune in to your instinct. Even though it's anything but a perfect wellspring of data, our abilities can frequently sift through issues more rapidly than a cognizant idea can.

This will permit you to settle on definitive decisions in troublesome circumstances.

3. Continuously Keep A Positive Attitude

Keep in mind the estimation of an inspirational mentality toward accomplishing your objectives. Regardless of the way you follow, it very well may be anything but difficult to get disheartened by brief mishaps or disappointments to achieve explicit objectives. Positive reasoning methods are recognizing these misfortunes as learning openings. This makes it simpler to beat little frustrations and keep endeavoring toward your goals.

Constructive reasoning likewise will, in general, make you an increasingly lovely person to be near, permitting you to draw in help from other people who can help you en route.

4. Make a move

You have to move your considerations without hesitation. Notwithstanding positive reviews, a mindset for progress additionally requires your speculation to be productive. At whatever point you are considering your objectives or obstructions to accomplishing them, you should have the option to recognize precise moves you can make accordingly.

The more promptly you can move a thought or want into a viable activity, the simpler it will be to gain ground toward your objectives.

5. Assume Complete Liability

A mindset for progress implies having the option to assume liability for all that you do, regardless of whether fortunate or unfortunate.

If you commit an error or mischief, somebody, along your way, assuming liability lets you contain the harm and save your notoriety. It likewise urges you to consider how you could stay away from that botch later on.

Similarly, if you achieve something, you need to guarantee duty regarding it. At exactly that point will others understand what you can do and bolster you on your way to progress.

Ways to Develop Your Mindset for Success

Top performers realize what they need and make a steady move towards it. They center on its most significant tasks. They persistently improve their abilities. Their smart personalities make passionate states, inspirations, and convictions that lead them to progress. Their mindsets direct them towards propensities and activities that produce their ideal outcomes.

1. Accept you'll succeed

Our conduct is steady with our convictions. If you accept you'll succeed, you make a successful move that draws you nearer to your objective. You assess the accessible choices in search of the most encouraging route forward. You persevere through difficulties since you're sure you will outperform them and proceed with the excursion towards progress.

Individuals respond contrastingly to comparable circumstances, dependent on their convictions. At the point when confronted with misfortune, one person comprehends it's a typical piece of the procedure while someone else whines that "things never go directly for me" and surrenders. The primary person developed a psychological structure that prompts a productive reaction to the misfortune.

If you accept there's a response to a problematic issue, you send your mindset to find that answer. You center on the conceivable outcomes and arrangements that will drive you forward. Then again, if you accept the issue is unsolvable, you direct your mind to locate the best reasons accessibly. Convictions direct our conduct. We can choose beliefs that push us towards our objectives rather than opinions that keep us down.

We will act reliably with our perspective on who we are, regardless of whether that view is precise or not.

2. Beat each snag in turn

At the point when we append to the result, we intellectually surge towards the end goal. Right now mind, we put an enormous focus on ourselves to succeed. We fixate on all the snags we may confront. We don't grasp gradual advancement and development. We need to track to the compensations of progress quickly. We can't viably deal with ten impediments without a moment's delay. Our psyche doesn't have the foggiest idea where to coordinate its consideration. Our consideration disperses, and our productive vitality disseminates.

We can beat each challenge in turn, however. We can systematically break down each challenge from all points. At that point, we can create procedures to assault the test in a manner that is well on the way to succeed. We focus on an arrangement and flood ahead. There's a long excursion ahead with numerous pinnacles and valleys. However, we don't have to discover answers for issues until we face them.

Separating the objective and concentrating exclusively on the following test is feasible. This mindset produces steady activity, which means monstrous advancement after some time.

3. Just contend with yourself

Displaying the mindsets, techniques, and activities of the individuals who have just achieved what we're seeking after is significant. Through demonstrating, we maintain a strategic distance from a portion of the missteps others made, making a course for progress. We find a demonstrated outline that abbreviates the time it takes us to arrive at our objectives. While gaining from others encourages our development, intellectually contending with them produces negative results. At the point when we measure ourselves against others, we look towards increasingly effective individuals. This leads us to feel deficient and question our capacity.

At the point when we move our ideal models and contend just with ourselves, we focus in on our way. We're not worried about what every other person is doing any longer. We're essentially attempting to improve from where we were yesterday. We're centered on enhancing our aptitudes and outfitting ourselves with the apparatuses we have to accomplish our objectives. We measure achievement dependent on our benchmarks rather than how others characterize achievement.

4. Focus on the best choices

As we become increasingly useful, we have more chances and demands. A of the open doors is great. If we express yes to most choices, we rapidly feel focused and overpowered by the volume of work and responsibilities. By disapproving of options that don't line up with our most significant objectives, we give ourselves the opportunity and space to entirely focus on the incredible preferences.

It's challenging to accomplish eager objectives. It's a lot harder to achieve these objectives when we have a lot on our plate. We gain steady ground on numerous undertakings without completing a large portion of them and betting everything on a couple of large ventures one after another until finish brings about gigantic movement. At the point when we finish them, we can proceed onward to the following arrangement of excellent choices that are pausing. We can accomplish all that we need. We can't accomplish everything simultaneously.

A business must include, it has some good times, and it needs to practice your innovative senses.

5. Build up a development mindset

Fruitful individuals have confidence in development. They accept their abilities will improve as they gain experience. They recognize they will discover guides, systems, and assets that will create the outcomes they need.

The development mindset prompts more outstanding commitment with challenges, perseverance, certainty, and eagerness to gain from botches. If we are confident that we will conquer these difficulties, we gain from them and continue attempting until we locate an effective strategy. The qualities related to a development mindset are a formula for progress.

At the point when we pick the development mindset over the fixed mindset, where we are today gets insignificant. The main thing that issues is the place we're going.

The Six Pillars of a Successful Mindset for Entrepreneurs

Being effective in business today is unique about it was ten years prior. As a business visionary, you are confronted with numerous difficulties and deterrents of the cutting edge age, including innovation to adjust to, web-based business to comprehend, and new and inventive approaches to secure clients. And these are advancing each day. Be that as it may, your ability to beat every one of these difficulties and to push ahead is basic to the accomplishment of your business. However, you have to sift through your psyche first.

The enterprise begins in your mind, and you need the correct mindset before you can develop an effective business. Find these six realities about the winning mindset that advances enterprise and discover what noteworthy characteristics can assist you with getting effective.

1. Positive Thinking

You can consider it an easy decision, yet this doesn't change the way that we have issues with it. A constructive clinician and hierarchical expert proclaim that "individuals will, in general, have a subjective inclination toward their disappointments, and pessimism." This implies human minds are bound to search out antagonism and assimilate it more rapidly to memory than actual data.

They state you can't accomplish your objectives without positive reasoning. Being sure is substantially more than merely being upbeat, and uplifting mentality that produces feelings, for example, satisfaction and happiness can make genuine incentive in your life and assist you with building aptitudes that last any longer than only a grin.

Your inspiration is both the antecedent to progress and its aftereffect. It has been demonstrated that the effect of positive feelings on the cerebrum causes you to feel and see more prospects throughout your life. Besides, positive reasoning will upgrade your capacity to assemble aptitudes and create assets to utilize further down the road.

So as should be obvious, positive reasoning and positive feelings help with enterprise, however your whole life as well. In any case, you can get yourself together and take a shot at your personality to change your perspective. Somewhat, you can get this going by overseeing zones of shortcoming to at long last increment the positive speculation in your life. For this attempt contemplation, expound on the positive experiences that you possess every day and calendar some energy for play and fun routinely.

OK, so we realize that positive reasoning is basic here; however, we should jump into different fundamentals of the business visionary's mindset.

2. Sensible Approach

Keep in mind; no one anticipates that you should transform into an unadulterated self-assured person who takes a gander at only the good in everything. Being practical is sufficient here.

Best business visionaries aren't hopeful in any way. They keep a sound separation in the tranquil occasions, and they don't get overexcited when everything functions admirably, and they are alarmed continuously and prepared for the war times so that you should simply change your approach and discover that there is no strength when you're growing a business.

3. You Must Be a Visionary Leader

Consider good examples, for example, the authority of Nelson Mandela, Henry Ford, or Alexander the Great. Despite the distinctive life purposes and missions they had, would they say they weren't all persuading in their dealings?

They were all visionaries. These are the best instances of visionary pioneers throughout the entire existence of humanity. Without the vision and the feeling of direction, defining a durable objective that everybody can move in the course of would not be conceivable.

Each pioneer needs enthusiasm about his specific plan to get sound. A business visionary isn't merely somebody who begins an organization for starting the organization, yet the individual takes care of a current issue. Here, each progression towards improvement and development is motivated by the incredible vision and desire for advancement.

At any rate, it should look that way. Visionary pioneers know their strategic feel it's solid calling from the time they were conceived. They ought to be able to look forward into the future more distant than others, foresee drifts and have a steadfast spotlight on an objective that may be accepted by others to be inconceivable.

At long last, they should attempt to push their plan as far as possible. At the point when you are a business person that drives a tech startup, and you effectively procure individuals for your group, you would do well to be a visionary. Having energy that means an away from of your organization structure is imperative to persuade individuals to go along with you and battle for the thought.

Since you can't persuade somebody regarding thought or business procedure when you don't have one, at the point when that is the situation, the best masters will detect it rapidly, and they will flee from you. We need those visionary heads to make products and administrations that carry an improvement to the world, and carry genuine incentive to individuals and tackle existing issues.

4. You Must Be a Persistent Leader

"Ability, virtuoso, and instruction mean next to no when persistence is inadequate."

Everything lies in proper assurance. The discourse was to show the need for persistence when attempting to accomplish goal-oriented or even unthinkable objectives. Persistence is the principal righteousness of the innovative mindset and one of the most basic factors in progress. An extraordinary achievement only from time to time comes without the exertion, and a lot of assurance.

Regularly the distinction between the individuals who succeed and the individuals who didn't lie in having the persistence to continue standing when everything else breakdown. It's anything but difficult to be persistent when all is well. Yet, we talk here about being persistent in the hours of an emergency when nothing is working out in a good way when the way is troublesome, and an answer isn't self-evident, and you appear not to draw near to your objectives by any means.

Persistence is the capacity to push ahead after a disappointment and having the internal certainty that encourages you to stand firm, prop up when it pours, defeat the snags and endure it until the minute when the sun turns out. It may get tested, yet it never gets annihilated; thus can generally go about as a wellspring of assurance and self-control to point higher and consistently seek after the advancement.

5. Consistent Learner

Million-dollar pioneers must output the world for signs of progress, and have the option to respond in a split second since this world progressively requires searchlight knowledge.

Searchlight knowledge is pivotal to envision what is coming straightaway and prevail with regards to developing prospects.

Therefore, nowadays, the best business people and pioneers become the best students. They should remain alert and constantly hungry for new information, abilities, and thinking designs that enable them to extend the scope of devices they use to gain the ideal ground and change or make what's to come. The best chiefs are normally interested and engaged with gaining from others, particularly the individuals who have just strolled a comparative way.

While perusing books isn't sufficient, you need genuine models and good solid examples. There is no better method to figure out how to turn into a fruitful business person than to gain from tutors, genuine, capable business visionaries. It's fundamental to encircle yourself with more intelligent individuals than yourself who can rouse you to turn out to be better and show the correct methods for beating difficulties and hindrances in your way.

6. Allure in Leadership

Martin Luther King Jr., Mahatma Gandhi, and Winston Churchill were known as unique, appealing, and helpful pioneers, and we expect this was an establishment of their achievement in authority.

All in all, what precisely comprises being a magnetic pioneer?

Appealing pioneers are extraordinary communicators that are outstandingly verbally expressive and fit for conveying on a profound, passionate level, contacting and stimulating forceful feelings in individuals.

They give the individuals around them a positive inclination, causing them to feel slanted to work with and adhere to guidance. Alluring pioneers are equipped for intriguing and motivating individuals around them and usually work admirably at advancing their ideas, associations, or manifestations.

The main concern

How about we abridge the six credits fundamental to a mindset of any practical business visionary.

These are, individually:

1. Positive reasoning that lets you make open doors for development and confidence in your favorable luck

2. A sensible methodology that gives you a sound perspective regardless of what occurs

3. A solid vision that pulls in individuals to battle for your thoughts

4. Persistence that pushes you ahead when everything else breakdown

5. Alertness to change and the insight to envision what is coming straightaway

6. The charisma that gives everyone around you a positive vibe to unite them.

7. On these occasions, while turning into a business visionary has gotten so natural, those mainstays of an enterprising mindset are considerably more essential than any time in recent memory since they let you recognize the genuine business people from the phony ones.

Furthermore, regardless of whether you're battling to turn into a business person yourself or you are merely hoping to unite with a characteristic head, consistently search out these highlights both in yourself and in others since they will guarantee the durable and superb initiative that expanded the likelihood to make progress you long for.

CHAPTER FIVE

HOW TO FIND THE WINNING PRODUCT

You have distinguished your market and niche. You have found out about the market and niche, have done some statistical surveying on the premiums and issues individuals have right now you have picked.

Presently the time has come to

1. Find out who the most significant players as far as products are right now;

2. Check out what they offer;

3. Choose among the contribution the product or administration you like and generally feel good with and

4. Optimize this for your prosperity!

Finding the principal players is very simple as it is sufficient to type in your fundamental keyword phrase into Google and see what natural outcomes spring up. Thus, if we picked as a model the market niche of skiing and have chosen to begin with the sub-niche and part of "head protectors for skiing," this is actually what you would type into Google to discover the main online deals point for ski caps.

When all is said in done, talking about products, you have to make an understood distinction between physical products (as the protective caps in the above model) and data products. Regularly online marketers incline toward offering data products mostly. This has a couple of reasons:

1. You don't need to keep any stock;

2. You don't need to fret over coordinations nor expenses of sending the products to individuals;

3. People can get their buy quickly, by just downloading (in a large portion of the cases) what they had requested;

4. It is quick and convenient: it may take you even US$15k to make a data product, yet once it is done, ready for action, there is fundamentally no more cost included - so it turns out to be profoundly gainful to you and your business.

A few niches may, however, demand physical products to advertise; you may have your creation, which is a physical product. Gain from the best in your niche to perceive how they oversee it and become much more useful than they are.

Be it a physical or a data product that you picked, make a point to

1. Find the enormous players in your niche;

2. opt-in to their rundown;

3. Read and check all they have;

4. Make a rundown of the considerable number of things you like and what doesn't speak to you;

5. Buy from them if conceivable or if nothing else consider doing as such;

6. Do a little market test before settling on one specific product or administration and a nitty-gritty marketing plan and technique to run.

Creating an Irresistible Product That Sells Like Crazy

Product creation is one of the most significant advances online that you have to ace to manufacture an active web business. The purpose behind this is to pick up the influence that you have to succeed; you need your products.

Right now might want to impart to your procedures to make products that will sell quite well.

1) Offer serious estimating

Particularly today, with the downturn and high oil costs, individuals are less ready to go through as a lot of cash as in the past. Thus it is significant that your costs offer worth. I recommend that you test various values to see which changes over the best. Here and there, a particular price will change over very well far superior to another, and you have to discover which one it is.

2) Add extra rewards

Regularly you will get individuals who will shift back and forth. You have to get them to make a move. You can do this by offering significant rewards. A strategy that numerous fruitful marketers use is they offer bonuses that appear to be more significant than the first product. Regularly individuals who are not yet chosen will follow up on the idea as the time touchy rewards will be a decent motivating force to buy it.

3) Offer your rival's extraordinary selling suggestion as a little something extra

In a severe market, it tends to be exceptionally hard to succeed. If you are battling to sell units of your product, I recommend that you include your rival's novel selling suggestion as a little something extra. Your purchaser will get a great deal of significant worth for cash, and this will swing things into your kindness.

Ways to Find Winning Products Every Time

What to offer, what to offer, what to sell. That is probably the most significant inquiry you'll be posing to yourself when fabricating your online store. How do a few hides away up, causing six and seven figures while others have a significant, fat zero? It comes down to having winning products. What's more, luckily, you should simply discover one to become wildly successful. So right now, going to answer a typical outsourcing FAQ: "How might I locate a triumphant product?" I separate the eight most straightforward approaches to discover such (and the specific thing that helped me locate my triumphant product)—time to get those dollar bills you all.

Most online stores have blockbuster records. This is incredible for clients who need to see the best products an online store can offer. Yet, for online retailers, smash hit singles are a cracking goldmine.

What's more, new business people don't misuse them enough.

Most express that the drawback to outsourcing is that everybody is selling indistinguishable products from you. In any case, I like to take a gander at it with a glass half full methodology: if everybody's selling similar stuff, you can undoubtedly sell it as well. Furthermore, if you comprehend what their smash hits are, at that point, you can sell a triumphant product. To discover the product that causes you to hit the bonanza, all you have to do is a tad of serious research.

Here are a couple of instances of websites with open success records.

1. Amazon Best Sellers

Along these lines, I will be a Captain Obvious and start with the conspicuous decision first.

Amazon has blockbuster records for truly every classification. That, however, they're refreshed each. Single. Hour.

You will discover some brand name products on success records like Lego and FujiFilm above. Nonetheless, you can likewise find some unbranded products that are additionally effectively accessible.

2. Wish's Winning Products

Wish is another case of an online retailer who plugs their top of the line products. Investigate the feline towels on the base right corner. More than 50,000 individuals have paid those towels off Wish's website, so they're certainly a triumphant product.

The cool thing about this feline towel is that you can quickly tell just from taking a gander at it that it's a spur of the moment purchase product. The more significant part of the triumphant products on Wish are obliged to pull in the spur of the moment purchase. So they usually would excel in visual stages like Facebook and Instagram.

So when glancing through smash hit records, keep your eyes open for spur of the moment purchase products. A few trademarks for spur of the moment purchase products incorporate things like:

Beautiful (or outwardly stands apart while looking over)

Evokes a passionate response ("I need this" or "This is lovable" or "I love this")

Diverse plan or style from anything you've at any point seen

3. Addition Your Competitor Here

The more significant part of your rivals has success records. Look at them. Regardless of whether you can't locate their precise product, by considering their product assortments, search for designs inside top of the line products.

In case you're in design, online retailer Suzy Shier has a patterns class. Inside the patterns class, you'll discover smash hits. In any case, similarly as intriguing that they likewise separate their apparel into style patterns. This can help give you a thought of what sorts of designs inside the style niche are mainstream at present. Under models, you see classifications like athleisure, creature prints, and plaid. In this way, you can search for design inside those sorts of ratings, so you're selling the most recent patterns.

Ardene is another retailer that has a patterns area. Sufficiently smart, when you look at their blockbusters, the primary thing that shows up is a plaid hoodie, which affirms that this pattern is ablaze at this moment. So in case, you're hoping to sell ladies' design, having a couple of plaid things can assist you with getting a few deals.

The more you glance through contender websites, the more you'll discover examples and associations among top brands. You can consolidate these examples as you construct your product assortment.

4. eBay Watch Count

Discover the product you should sell utilizing Watch Count, which permits you to perceive what's famous on eBay. You can either discover winning products on hyper-focused on catchphrases like 'ionic hairbrush' to see the photographs and style that is most well known at present.

Or on the other hand, you can expand your catchphrases so you can locate the hits in your niche. So rather than an ionic hairbrush, you'd simply search hairbrush. Or, on the other hand, rather than blossom stockings, you'd simply search tights.

The best things to outsource are the ones recorded with the most watchers. Remember that while doing a restricted search like an ionic hairbrush, the number of watchers will be lower since you're explicit and that the ionic hairbrush is still uncontrollably mainstream, notwithstanding a smaller amount than the tights.

Likewise, you'll notice that with the two arrangements of pictures that there are always numerous products that appeared to see. Making your photographs along these lines can also assist clients with seeing the whole determination before clicking onto your product page (and it can help tempt them more since there are more alternatives for them to see).

5. Screen High-Performing Ads

We live in a universe of scrollers. We look through articles, newsfeeds, and product pages. Be that as it may, have you at any point halted to figure what could occur if you didn't look past a perpetual flood of posts?

My reality changed because, at some point, I quit looking to take a gander at a Facebook advertisement.

Yet, in some way or another, the promotion commitment on this triumphant product was not normal for anything I'd at any point seen before, demonstrating that it was probably the best thing to outsource. High as can be. Many remarks. Companion labeling like you wouldn't accept—a vast number of preferences.

Everybody needed this product.

It was practically difficult to accept that these remarks were genuine. In any case, they were.

I chose to search for a comparable product with Oberlo. It was a significant, brilliant cover, so I attempted various catchphrases like "seashore cover" and "reflection cover." After a touch of searching, I found the specific, same product.

6. Unicorn Smasher

Are you searching for an Amazon product research instrument? Unicorn Smasher encourages you to locate the top of the line Amazon products for nothing. With this convenient Chrome expansion, you can discover the costs, smash hit rank, surveys, appraisals, and assessed deals in a solitary look. What's more, this information appears for every Amazon product insofar as you're on the .com area.

How about we investigate the information while searching for kitchen products. You can decide to sort any of the Chrome augmentations by any of its headers. Here I chose to see dependent on assessed income, yet you can likewise see by value, rank, surveys, appraisals, and whether it's satisfied by Amazon.

A convenient stunt for dropshippers to locate the best things to outsource is to see dependent on the number of venders. If there are various dealers for a single product, the product can be found on AliExpress. For instance, if iRobot Roomba just has one merchant and you see that iRobot is additionally the brand name, you likely won't have the option to sell the product since it's marked. Nonetheless, numerous merchants show that the product probably isn't marked, and anybody can sell it as well.

7. Utilizing Oberlo to Find the Product

Inside Oberlo, you can gain admittance to information for different AliExpress products. You can discover which products have had deals and which haven't. Be that as it may, you can likewise see how later those deals are. Is it safe to say that they were in the previous 30 days or the last half-year?

How about we peruse the watchword neckband. While perusing accessory, we can discover request volume by clicking "Request check" in the dropdown adjacent to "Sort by."

At the base, you'll see product measurements. You'll need to take a gander at all of these subtleties to assist you with settling on a choice. The 4.7-star rating is extraordinary. I usually prefer to remain above 4.5 stars. However, remember that if there are more than 100 audits, anything over a 4 star is an excellent product to browse.

Imports disclose to you what number of others are selling winning products like this one. With regard to site visits, I like to contrast it and request from the most recent 30 days. At the point when you isolate orders from the previous 30 days against total online visits (likewise from the last 30 days), take a gander at the percentage you get. If it's above half, you likely have a triumphant product on your hands. Anything lower than that and your advertisement evaluating may wind up costing you to an extreme.

With regards to Orders, verify whether the requests in the previous 30 days are high. If they're taller than the last a half year, you likely got it before the pattern exploded. You don't have to dishonor an excellent product given it either. This heart accessory, despite everything, got 2500+ deals in the previous 30 days that is still madly high. Regardless of whether the pattern is kicking the bucket, you can even now profit by it if deals in the previous 30 days are in the hundreds or higher.

8. Step by step instructions to Use Google Trends to Find Winning Products

Google Trends is a famous free instrument you can use to see whether a product is developing or declining in fame. Peruse this to discover an inside and out breakdown about how to utilize Google Trends to find winning products. Be that as it may, meanwhile, we should separate some fundamental thoughts on the most proficient method to discover the product utilizing this device.

Utilizing Google Trends, enter the product type. For instance, a popular AliExpress product is a rose in a glass that you can sell as wedding focal points, a Valentine's Day blessing, or a piece for the home stylistic theme. I include "rose in glass" to see the search volume prominence and presto.

How to discover winning products to sell on Shopify?

Tips no 1:

Ensure that your product page has in any event 400 words on it. Something to remember when you're making your website Google inviting is that Google is a robot, a machine. It comprehends the best is numbers and content.

At the point when Google sees you have heaps of elegantly composed content on your product page, shows to them you care about, giving your client an extraordinary experience. Eventually, Google has one objective, and that is to take care of its clients' issues. So when you're putting heaps of words on your page, it shows to them that is what you're attempting to utilize bunches of distinct applicable terms.

Tips no 2:

Shop assess

We're taking a gander at here is a website called shop assess. We're taking a gander at the hot products segment. We simply take one product. For instance, we take a Wi-Fi IP camera named the child screen. It is an approach to screen your resting infant from your genuine cell phone. So this is an excellent product that we may sell.

You can see that it's indeed expanded. What we will do is we will make sense of how to focus on this awful kid and send ethics to this product that will be intrigued enough to purchase this product. So what we will do is we will head into audience bits of knowledge.

Audience bits of knowledge resembles a cheat sheet for Facebook Ads. Again Facebook Ads has more than two billion month to month dynamic clients. So your purchasers are on Facebook regardless of what product you sell. There are 55% ladies, 45% men.

Presently if individuals who are keen on child screens, 90% percent are ladies, just 10% are men. We can likewise observe significantly further cheat codes by seeing what different pages of individuals who are keen on infant screens.

We can go out and target individuals out there who are ladies. We saw that 90% of individuals who are keen on child screens are ladies. Not a great deal of men are going out there and purchasing child screens. So we will target just ladies.

Etsy

Etsy is an online commercial center only like Amazon, eBay, with outsider vendors. It's an immense wellspring of deals and traffic with more than 35 million dynamic purchasers on the stage. I like it for novices. It's strangely modest to list things. They're only 20 pennies for an entire month posting with a small deals charge.

This article is tied in with directing people to a Shopify store, not an Etsy store. You can do what I did when propelled my first useful online store at the young age of 16. I would show some popular products from outsider commercial centers and develop a nearness on there. You would guide those clients to your store.

Tips no 3:

Presently we will hop into a hot website. We will type in everybody does it directly here into a help called SEM surge. If we press search semrush will let us know is the place precisely their traffic is originating from. If you are keen on various things, it will be distinctive every time for you. So we will come into the SEM surge. We will type in the space of a website we know an online business store; that we know is detonating in prominence at present.

The most underutilized paid to promote stage right currently is Instagram. Particularly if you are utilizing video advertisements on the scene, and they are performing better than Facebook. As you look through an Instagram feed, you notice the ads in it.

CHAPTER SIX

WHICH MARKETING CHANNELS TO USE

A marketing channel is the individuals, associations, and exercises essential to move the responsibility for from the purpose of production to the point of utilization. It is how products find a workable pace client, the shopper, and is otherwise called an appropriation channel.

Kinds of Marketing Channels

There are fundamentally four kinds of marketing channels:

1. Direct selling;

2. Selling through go-betweens;

3. Dual dissemination;

4. Reverse channels.

Direct Selling

Direct selling is the marketing and sale of products straightforwardly to shoppers from a fixed retail store. Hawking is the most seasoned type of direct selling. Present-day direct selling incorporates deals made through the gathering plan, one-on-one shows, and personal contact courses of action just as web deals. The immediate personal introduction, exhibit, and offer of products and administrations to buyers, for the most part, in their homes or at their occupations.

Purchasers profit by direct selling given the comfort and administration benefits it provides, including personal exhibition and clarification of products, home conveyance, and liberal fulfillment ensures. Rather than diversifying, the expense for a person to begin a free immediate selling business is commonly low, with almost no necessary stock or money responsibilities to start.

Direct selling is not quite the same as direct marketing in that it is about individual deals operators coming to and managing customers while direct marketing is about business associations looking for a relationship with their clients without experiencing a specialist/expert or retail outlet.

Direct selling frequently, however not generally, utilizes staggered marketing (a salesperson is paid for selling and for deals made by individuals they select or support) as opposed to single-level marketing (salesperson is paid uniquely for the business they make themselves).

Selling Through Intermediaries

A marketing channel where middle people, for example, wholesalers and retailers, are used to making a product accessible to the client is called a roundabout channel. The most aberrant pathway you can utilize (Producer/maker – > specialist – > distributer – > retailer – > customer) is used when there are numerous little makers and various small retailers, and an operator is utilized to help arrange an enormous stock of the product.

Double Distribution

Double conveyance depicts a wide assortment of marketing courses of action by which the producer or wholesalers utilizes more than one channel all the while to arrive at the end client. They may sell legitimately to the end clients just as offer to different organizations for resale. Utilizing at least two channels to draw in a similar objective market can, in some cases, lead to channel strife.

A case of double dissemination is business group diversifying, where the franchisors, permit the operation of a portion of its units to franchisees while at the same time owning and operating a few units themselves.

Switch Channels

If you've found out about the other three channels, you would have seen that they make them thing in like manner — the stream. Every one streams from maker to middle person (if there is one) to purchaser.

Innovation, nonetheless, has made another stream conceivable. This one goes in the turn around bearing and may go — from buyer to delegate to the recipient. Consider bringing in cash from the resale of a product or reusing.

There is another qualification between turn around channels and the more conventional ones — the presentation of a recipient. In turning around the stream, you won't discover a maker. You'll just find a User or a Beneficiary.

Six Marketing Channels You Can Prioritize in 2020

1. Pay-Per-Click Marketing

To the extent marketing channels go, pay-per-click (PPC) publicizing is as yet an incredible juggernaut, particularly with the differing alternatives now accessible to brands. There is a high expectation to consume information for every stage, so if you can bear to enlist an organization to deal with your battles for you, we prescribe that.

There are two overwhelming powers in the PPC world nowadays: Google Ads and Facebook/Instagram Ads. Google search promotions will assist you with associating with clients who are searching for products or administrations like yours.

In the interim, Google's showcase advertisements and Facebook's paid social promotions will permit you to make the request and acquaint your administrations with clients who may not be looking or even realize you exist.

You can become familiar with how to take advantage of Google Ads here and Facebook Ads here.

2. Online networking

Online networking is a significant player in the marketing scene at this moment. Clients are effectively searching out brands they like or are keen on, and expanding quantities of clients are taking to online networking to research or settle on purchasing choices.

Internet-based life additionally offers relevant network building openings that you indeed won't find anyplace else. Regardless of whether you're merely sharing in the background content on your page or making a gathering, including your business, you ought to use internet-based life for everything it has.

3. Email Marketing

Email marketing is the best technique for direct reaction marketing there is. Clients have selected into got notification from you, so they're all the more ready to open those messages to find out about the most recent products, deals, and how to profit by them. Email marketing can be perplexing, so we've canvassed it inside and out here.

4. Your Website

A few businesses don't think about their website as a marketing channel, yet as a general rule, it might be the most significant one. This is the place clients will come when they're keen on becoming familiar with your business, and if they can't discover answers to their inquiries rapidly, they won't stay sufficiently long to see. Your site should offer a decent early introduction, and it ought to speak to your business, image, products, and administrations in the manner in which you need it.

5. Content Marketing and SEO

Content marketing is somewhat similar to an investment account. Over the long haul, you get intensifying enthusiasm, making it considerably increasingly important. The posts can offer SEO benefits for an exceptionally prolonged period to come as individuals keep on searching them out, and the entirety of your substance can give significant relationship building and lead age capacities. Content marketing shows authority and expertise, all while helping you arrive at clients at various phases of the channel and hitting the same number of catchphrases as you can.

6. Informal Marketing

Informal marketing has consistently been one of the best marketing channels, and that will proceed on an on-going premise. You'll get over it if a salesperson discloses to you that you need that watch, however when your companion calls attention to the amount they love wearing it consistently on account of all the bright highlights, you'll take more notification.

There are two essential strategies to empower verbal marketing. Referral projects and rousing on the web surveys for various stages of web-based, including Google, LinkedIn, and Yelp.

CHAPTER SEVEN

HOW MUCH MONEY IT TAKES TO GET STARTED

Affiliate Marketing (AM) is a business, and similarly, as with some other activity, you have to put away some cash toward the start. Individuals continue asking how a lot of money is expected to begin in AM and whether it's even conceivable with a little spending plan. So let me investigate this point, to enable you to comprehend the stuff to turn into an affiliate marketer regarding financing.

As a matter of first importance, we have to sort one thing out – to sell anything by any stretch of the imagination, you need the guests (traffic), and there are two potential ways to deal with getting it – PAID and FREE (natural). The straightforward rationale behind these two methodologies decides how much $ you will need to begin. If you choose to work with PAID traffic, your costs will be higher, obviously.

This is clear and straightforward. Be that as it may, to honestly choose what approach would be better for you, we have to jump into this somewhat deeper. The two methodologies have their upsides and downsides, so let me attempt to think about them.

Stars of Paid Traffic:

– You can begin getting guests promptly, everything necessary is to make a record at some traffic source, finance your career, make a crusade, and dispatch it. You may need to stand by some an opportunity to get your campaigns affirmed. However, that is typically only several hours.

– You choose how much traffic you will purchase. If you have the financial limit for this, solitary anything is possible. This is the highest favorable position of the "paid" approach – when you have a crusade that works, you can open the conduits and begin making 1000s of $$$ per day. Improving efforts isn't simple, yet it truly can work this way. Super affiliates who run a massive amount of volume per day, usually are working with paid traffic.

– You choose what traffic you will purchase and who you get it from. Suppose you have an incredible product. However, it just acknowledges guests from Austria, they must peruse on a Samsung SmartPhone, and they should be associated through the Orange portable bearer? This isn't an issue with paid traffic; you can pick precisely what sort of traffic you need to purchase.

– You needn't bother with any site to purchase traffic. It's not as simple as it was previously, yet you can at present bring in cash by sending guests straightforwardly to the product pages, without keeping up any site of your own.

Masters of Free (Organic) Traffic:

– Well, it's free: This is the highest favorable position of this methodology. You will, in any case, need to make some minor ventures and invest a ton of your energy in it. However, the traffic itself is free. Produce content that individuals might want, and the guests will come to you in the end.

– Free natural traffic will, in general, be increasingly steady, it won't bite the dust starting with one day then onto the next.

Except if you get prohibited by google, for instance, so center on whitehat techniques for traffic building.

– Organic traffic is generally of high, discover something that your guests are keen on, and they will change over. You can likewise offer this traffic to some traffic networks or individual purchasers.

– Since you need a website to get natural traffic, you are constructing a benefit that can transform into an automated revenue source. When a site is positioned, everything necessary is to refresh it now and again, and it can continue bringing in cash for quite a long time. My longest running site was begun in 2003, and it is as yet bringing in money, 13 years in a row! Building locales dependent on natural traffic can likewise be a piece of your leave procedure; you would have something to sell.

Let me start with PAID traffic again:

– A higher spending plan is required. Since you have to purchase all the traffic, you need the financial limit for it. Without a doubt, the base I would suggest would be $1000. If you don't have this sort of cash, paid traffic isn't for you, not yet. You have to assemble the spending limit somewhere else first, perhaps even with natural traffic. Traffic isn't the main cost: you will likewise require a server, domain(s), following arrangement, spy tool ... I will summarize it somewhat later on.

– You will free cash from the outset, and this is entirely inescapable. Every one who, at any point, began with paid traffic was losing money from the start. If you figure you will be unique, you are incorrect. PERIOD! This is something you have to acknowledge, in any case, don't begin with paid traffic.

– You should manage some degree of misrepresentation – traffic networks sell bots, affiliate networks clean leads ... these are irritations you need to become accustomed to. We as a whole need to manage that; no one is resistant to this, so it's not something just you'd need to battle with. Simply required to take note of that.

– You can lose a great deal of cash! Reconsider before settling on any choice, watch your battles intently, and utilize all means imaginable to restrain your drops.

– There are no ensures that you will make it. Not every person has the correct mindset or aptitudes to make it with paid traffic. Try not to feel that since you contribute $1000, you are ensured to begin making benefits. Numerous individuals come up short at this. However, on the other hand, it's equivalent to a business.

– Running paid traffic is magnificent when all clicks fine and dandy, yet it very well may be super unpleasant when it's most certainly not. When testing new products, sources ... that is no joke "not bringing in cash" you are losing it. This is again something you need to become accustomed to.

Free Traffic Has Cons Too:

– You have to run content destinations to assemble natural traffic by any means. Regardless of whether you decide to concentrate on SEO (search engine optimization), Viral locales, or Social media, you will consistently need to manufacture substance to pull in the guests.

– You have to put a great deal of time into your locales; somebody needs to compose/produce the substance. You can likewise employ somebody to do it for you, yet this will drive your expenses up a ton. You additionally need to refresh your locales to safeguard your search engine rankings for a more extended period.

– It takes any longer to fabricate natural traffic contrasted with utilizing paid promotions. As a rule, you have to create content for quite a long time without getting a lot of guests. It's anything but difficult to surrender and quit delivering content when nobody is taking a gander at it.

– When building SEO traffic, you are necessarily Google's bitch. What google gives, google can take. Since they claim such a massive % of the market, if they boycott you, your site is done.

– Organic traffic is a blend of GEOs (nations), traffic types (portable, tablet, work area), and so forth ... this makes it somewhat harder to adapt every hit. You can't generally make uncommon ADs for each language that your guests talk, and visits from individual nations will be simply squandering your Bandwidth bill since they originate from countries that no one need's to promote/sell in.

I could go on with the PROS and CONS, yet I would state the most significant has been secured, and I'm sure you, as of now, comprehend the principle contrasts. If I summarized it in one sentence, it would be something like this: Working with **PAID** traffic requires a way higher spending plan, and you can consume a ton of $ with it. However, the potential benefits are more top as well, and you can begin immediately. Natural traffic can return progressively stable benefits, yet for the most part, in the lower range and get ready to manufacture content for a considerable length of time before observing any profits.

So How Much Money Do You Need To Start With Either Of Them?

Let me attempt to summarize the inescapable expenses related to beginning in AM, both with paid and natural (free) traffic.

PAID Traffic First:

— You need some facilitating to put greeting pages (LPs) on, and you can attempt without LPs as well. However, you will begin utilizing presentation pages in the end, at any rate. When starting, you can pick a modest VPS or Cloud arrangement from organizations like beyondhosting.com, vultr.com, or digitalocean.com ... I hope to spend anyplace between $20 and $50 per month, in light of what plan you pick.

There is a considerable amount of hosts so pick anything you desire, yet remember a specific something — with paid traffic; speed is a significant factor, you need every click that you purchased, to hit your points of arrival. Try not to go for shared facilitating like bluehost.com, hostgator.com, and so on ... these are modest, yet they are not reasonable for paid traffic battles.

If you utilize static (Html just) LPs, you can likewise use a CDN, rackspace.com cloud petitions, for instance. These are charged per GB moved. LPs usually are extremely "light" pages so that it will be practically free. I'm paying under $5 per month, and I'm serving 100s of thousands of hits per day. It will rely upon the KB size of your LPs.

– You additionally need TRACKING; this is an absolute necessity. With paid traffic, it's significant to know precisely what sort of traffic changed over to purchase a more considerable amount of that. What's more, this is tracker's main event; they will show you precisely what guest made a change – what site/arrangement they originate from, what nation, what gadget ...

There are many trackers out there. However, some of them are viewed as the best ones. We had a survey on STM Forum in the relatively recent past, and these five turned out as champs: Voluum, Thrive Tracker, FunnelFlux, Adsbridge, and CPV Lab.

Every one of them is charged on a per month premise, except CPV Lab, which is a one time charge. Some are self-facilitated, which implies you need to utilize your server or CPV for this: CPV Lab and Funnel Flux. The remainder of them is facilitated and Thrive both a facilitated and a self-facilitated adaptation.

Voluum begins at $99 per month for 1.000.000 occasions. 10.000.000 occasions plan is $399.

Flourish begins at $99 per month for oneself facilitated variant and $299 for the facilitated one.

FunnelFlux is a level $99 per month, per permit. The offer just a self-facilitated adaptation for the present, so you need your server as well.

CPV Lab is a onetime charge of $297, which incorporates one year of help and updates. Extra help is discretionary and costs $147 per year. This needs a server again, too, as it's a self-facilitated tracker.

Asbridge offers a free essential arrangement for up to 50.000 visits per month. This is a low cutoff, so it's just useful for the initial hardly any days, the following arrangement comes at $25 for 100.000 visits. 1.000.000 visits plan is $75 per month.

Every one of the trackers has a few advantages and disadvantages, so it's difficult to prescribe one, however, let me attempt it in any case. FunnelFlux gets my vote if you need a self-facilitated tracker, it has a lot of decent choices. Voluum is most likely the best-facilitated tracker, yet it gets costly with high volume. That is the place Thrive takes over as their high volume plans are increasingly moderate. Asbridge is a well-known decision among amateurs, on account of the free essential arrangement, yet with higher volume, the costs grow up to a similar level similarly as with rivalry.

– The next thing you MUST have is a VPN (Virtual Private Network) programming. The most famously known is HideMyAss.Com. What this delicate does is concealing your whole area and supplanting your IP address with one of their private ones. Along these lines, you can surf the net as though you were associated with any nation on the planet.

This is valuable when you need to check what your opposition is advancing in any given GEO of the world. Since basically, all traffic networks use GEO focusing on, you just observe ADs targeted at your nation, except if you counterfeit it with a VPN.

– if you can bear the cost of it, I would prescribe to get a spy tool as well. I utilize the Adplexity group of apparatuses; they have separate devices for versatile, local, grown-up, and work areas. Having a spy tool is certainly not an absolute must. However, it unquestionably helps a TON.

These apparatuses "surf" the web and gather Intel pretty much a wide range of contenders' battles, so you can without much of a stretch break down them in one spot. Along these lines, you know precisely what is advanced where … right from standard, through the LP to the genuine product.

Outline For Paid Traffic:

Unquestionably the base is VPS ($20-$50 per month) or a CDN ($5 per month), tracker ($25 – $99 per month), VPN ($5-$15 per month) in addition to in any event $20-$30 per day for traffic. If you can manage the cost of it, including $150 per month for a spy tool. This implies, given the tracker and facilitating you pick, you need at any rate $635 for the first month. If you choose a VPS, the expense goes up to $655-$670. Picking an increasingly costly tracker will kick the costs up by another $75, so that would generally mean $750. Include a government agent device, and you are at $900.

To stand a reasonable possibility at succeeding, you need assets to cover at any rate three months. Indeed, even thou you will free from the start, some portion of the cash will return as far as income created (not benefit), so you needn't bother with a numerous of 3 to cover the initial three months. In any case, it would be a smart thought to get ready in any event $1500 – $2000, if you are not kidding about paid traffic AM.

Looking At Starting With Organic Traffic

As I previously referenced, not every person has the monetary allowance for working with paid traffic straight away. Numerous affiliates start with natural traffic, and once they develop their financial limit, they move to paid traffic. This is a generally excellent procedure as well. Also, it's lovely to have a side pay set up while walking into paid traffic – it assists with dealing with the pressure.

– The most significant factor here is TIME. Start now. It will take a long time to get a few positions in google and different SEs (search engines) to get saw via web-based networking media to fabricate content that can draw in guests. Try not to pause and start NOW. Try not to stress if you don't have a perfect arrangement; you can clean things as you go. You can resolve the little glitches later on, yet you unquestionably can't return to the past.

– You should construct a site or a network of locales. Check my more established post about structure, a system of small niche locales to get some motivation. You need a few CMS (content administration framework) to run a site. You have two choices here once more, either pick a costly one (or exceptionally coded) or pick a free one.

I firmly prescribe, to begin with, the free arrangements, the most well known are WordPress and Joomla. I like WordPress more, yet a few people incline toward the other one, so the decision is yours. These CMS frameworks are mainstream to the point that you can do nearly anything with them, even e-looks, for instance. Enthusiasts of the stage delivered a considerable amount of alleged "modules" that you can introduce and construct propelled destinations with.

These frameworks both utilize a TEMPLATE framework; formats are one of a kind structures/designs that you can download either for nothing or get them. The costs for entirely propelled arrangements start at around $20; there is a considerable amount of great ones at $40-$50. Look at TemplateMonster.Com. For instance, there is a fuckload of them to pick a structure.

– Domain or spaces – Pick something identified with the subject of your site(s), yet don't go through a month searching for the perfect area name. The significance of a space name is no place as large as it used to be. What's more, wtf is a "google"? They caused it to up, and now everybody comprehends what it speaks to, you can attempt the equivalent. You can pick up spaces for a couple of pennies with the assistance of Godaddy.Com coupons, for instance.

– You have to have the site(s) someplace. The necessities on facilitating speed are not all that exacting likewise with paid traffic, so even a mutual arrangement could carry out the responsibility. There are also some free has accessible, yet I'm not a fanatic of anything free – you get what you pay for. Get a modest VPS or a cloud arrangement, digitalocean.com or vultr.com ought to carry out the responsibility fine and dandy. However, any facilitating with not too bad audits will be sufficient to have a little site.

Start with a modest arrangement, and if you figure out how to develop, you can generally overhaul. The beneficial thing is, except if you intend to assemble free grown-up locales, you needn't bother with 10.000s of visits to make better than average income. Attempt to pick a subject that you are acceptable at and fabricate content dependent on your insight. Accept this blog, for instance, I'm acceptable at I's job, so I expound on it. For the individuals who might want to comprehend the stuff to assemble a site this way, I made a segment where I will present the month-on-month progress, look at it here.

– You ought to likewise manufacture an email list/pamphlet; there are many answers for this. You can utilize free modules for this once more, yet individuals, as a rule, arrive at better outcomes with paid instruments. There is a great deal of them: Aweber, Getresponse, Mailchimp ... these beginning at $15 - $20 per month and increment as your rundown develops.

There is a massive amount of different things that you could put resources into – like substance makers, coders, courses to show you how to do one or the other ... however, in all actuality, to START, you simply need an area, CMS framework, and a server + a considerable amount of your time.

Outline For Free (Organic) Traffic

How about we summarize the costs expected to begin "distributing" – Domain ($1-$10 per year), Hosting ($5-$20 per month), CMS (free), Template ($0-$50), Email Collection ($0-$15 per month). We are taking a gander at an underlying expense of under $10 if we figure out how to locate a modest area and utilize free modules at every possible opportunity.

If we choose to purchase a superior facilitating, propelled format, and a paid email list arrangement, the cost will go up to about $90 for the underlying mechanism (in addition to first month expenses) and afterward $35 per month. I don't know I think about whatever other business where you could begin THIS CHEAP!

I'd prefer to save your consideration for a couple of more seconds and reveal to you one more thing: if you are hoping to gain 1000's of $$$ per day, building locales for natural traffic is presumably not your last goal. Some regions make that sort of cash, and we, as a whole, know the anecdotes about websites or online administrations that sold for millions. However, the likelihood of this transpiring is VERY little.

Without a doubt, it can occur, yet it will take long stretches of challenging work and exceptional thought. The more typical path is, to begin with, natural traffic, develop the financial limit, and afterward move to paid traffic to raise the income.

Making enormous aggregates of cash is simpler with paid traffic. It's not straightforward using any means; however, if you figure out how to decipher the code, it's just a matter of a couple of months to begin making 100's of $$$ in a day by day benefits. I know a lot of individuals who make $10.000 – $15.000 benefit per month with paid traffic, and those are not the large mutts. Super affiliates make $1000s in profit per day, and some are sitting on the top who reach $10.000s or even six figures in benefits in a single day.

I am a major aficionado of a half and half methodology as it were. Having a couple of automated revenue natural traffic locales is the thing that keeps my psyche in harmony when my paid battles suck and lose cash. When the paid crusades assume control over, the significance of these destinations diminishes; it is only an additional salary that is pleasant to have. Be that as it may, since each paid crusade kicks the bucket sooner or later, the cycle begins once again and over.

Assemble destinations for dependability and ideally, to have something to sell when the need emerges. Remove a portion of the cash and put it into paid traffic and check whether you can make it there. Take the best from the two universes. You can likewise check this more seasoned article of mine to peruse progressively about the natural VS paid methodology.

The amount of Money Do You Need To Start Affiliate Marketing.

While it is conceivable, to begin with, affiliate marketing at for all intents and purposes no expense, if you need to prevail in the business and bring in some cash, you ought to be set up to go through some money first. Consider it an essential business venture. Here are the run of the mill costs you'll be taking a gander at if you need to set up your own business as an affiliate marketer.

Affiliate marketing costs

I expect that, since you understand this, you, as of now, have a PC that is associated with the web. So the following things you have to get your affiliate marketing business ready for action are:

An area name

You'll require a website. Furthermore, for that, you need a space name. You can enlist an area name with Namecheap for as meager as $4 per year.

Facilitating

You'll require someplace to have your new website on the web. Facilitating can be bought for as meager as $6-7 per month. Look at HostGator or pick an area and promoting bundle with Namecheap.

That is it. You're all set. Simply add substance and affiliate connects to your website, and you're presently an affiliate marketer.

Is it's as simple as that? You could stop there and not spend another dollar. Be that as it may, I recommend you continue perusing.

Discretionary Extras

I state discretionary, yet in case you're extremely genuine about your affiliate marketing business, these are an easy decision. A space name and website facilitating might be everything to getting a website. However, there's a whole other world to affiliate marketing than just having a website. Putting resources into a portion of the beneath will make your life simpler, and significantly improve your odds of having a fruitful affiliate marketing business.

Website design enhancement and Keyword Tools

Compelling catchphrase research is critical. You'll require this for your SEO (and PPC) endeavors. There are free watchword research instruments. However, some are justified even despite the cash you have to pay for them, for example, SEMRush, from $69.95 per month, which additionally offers a lot of investigation reports, and that's only the tip of the iceberg.

PPC

Done astutely, Google's paid promoting framework can give you an extraordinary profit for your venture. You set the sum you are eager to pay for each click your promotion gets. However, you'll likewise be contending with different sponsors who are offering on your catchphrases as well. So it tends to be very simple to become excited and spend too far in the red. So don't endeavor PPC except if you realize what you are doing first, else you'll be tossing cash down the channel.

Hope to pay on ordinary between 20-50p per click for known to medium serious niches, to 50p or more of severe slots. Plan an every day spending plan of around £10, although it's prudent to set aside a financial limit of about £100 ($150) with which you can test and decide if you are getting a decent profit for your speculation.

Email Marketing

Email marketing is a vital marketing instrument, empowering you to rapidly and effectively arrive at enormous quantities of potential clients. AWeber is the best. Contingent upon what number of endorsers you need, you'll be paying from $19 per month. However, you can attempt it free for 30 days first.

Pictures

If you need your website or blog and its substance to have an expert, quality look, you'll have to put resources into some stock photography because, because of copyright laws, you can't merely utilize any picture you need that you discovered on the web. Locales like Dreamstime empower you to purchase credits that can be used to pay for downloads. Loans for up to 11 pictures are accessible for under $10.

Redistributing

You can't hope to know it all about affiliate marketing, and all things considered, you can't expect to do everything yourself. So instead of attempting to do everything, eventually, you should get some assistance by re-appropriating some work. Enter the specialist. You can pay somebody who has what it takes and information that is missing to do anything from improving your website plan to make a change over substance for it.

Look at Elance and Upwork for consultants gaining practical experience in the aptitudes that you're inadequate. I hope to pay in any event $15 per hour/employment to significantly more, contingent upon the individual specialist and their experience.

Complimentary gifts You Can Use to Start Affiliate Marketing.

Fortunately, there are a lot of free apparatuses online that you can use to further your potential benefit. So take advantage of them.

Google Analytics

Each affiliate marketer needs Google Analytics. It's the best free examination administration accessible, and without it, you should be maintaining your affiliate marketing business visually impaired.

Google AdWords Keyword Planner

Albeit free, the Google AdWords Keyword Planner requires you to have an AdWords record to utilize it, which can be a problem in case you're not hoping to do any PPC. Be that as it may, it is, for the most part, viewed as the best, and will furnish you with some great details to go with your catchphrases, for example, rivalry level, average CPC and that's only the tip of the iceberg. Less problem, and still free, is Keyword Tool.io.

Preparing

Try not to squander your cash on books, guides, and costly affiliate marketing preparing. There is an abundance of data to be found uninhibitedly on the web and a lot of free preparing projects, for example, our Affiliate Training Course. Be that as it may, don't invest such a lot of energy attempting to get the hang of all that you can that you neglect ever to begin. Once in a while, the best learning strategy is to hop directly in and do it simply.

What are the fundamental costs when you are merely beginning an affiliate marketing

If you were to simply pay for the essential expenses of setting up a website, you could hope to spend under $10 per month. That is under $120 per year. Tiny right?

Be that as it may, your lucrative potential indeed relies upon whether you have the correct instruments.

So when you give some genuine thought to the immense contrast all – or even only a portion of those additional items above will put forth to your affiliate marketing attempts and the achievement you harvest from it, you'll understand that the other venture is well justified, despite all the trouble.

Ensure you have some income to begin, and just use the cash you can bear to lose. Since recollect, affiliate marketing, similar to any business, isn't an ensured approach to wealth!

CHAPTER EIGHT

PRACTICAL EXAMPLE

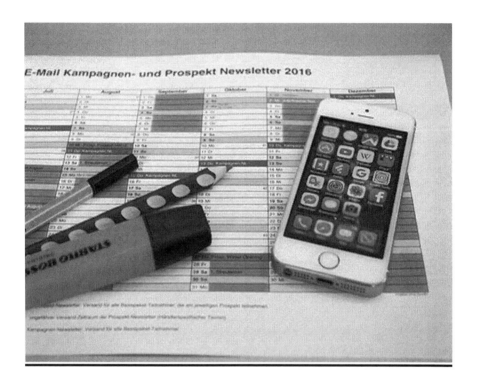

The most agent affiliate marketing models? Amazon and the locales 'consistently convey' and 'gear watch.'

Locales related to the Amazon affiliate program flourish, less for the commission earned yet for the assortment, security, and esteem of Jeff Bezos' internet business. Perhaps the best case of affiliate marketing procedures is Everyday Carry, a fascinating site of surveys of endurance articles.

In Everyday Carry, it is conceivable to discover investigations of Swiss Army Knives, watches, electric lamps, contraptions, knapsacks, note pads, and different products, which are vital in the baggage of the courageous open. Every one of their connections leads to Amazon products, where the buy is made. The equivalent occurs in Gear Patrol, a site that covers a more noteworthy number of products and market niches.

Rigging Patrol is another of Amazon's best instances of affiliate websites. It is characterized as an everyday men's magazine, gaining practical experience in movement, knowledge, nourishment, and innovation. Notwithstanding getting a great many daily visits, this site has a massive network of faithful adherents, who are diverted to Amazon through affiliate joins. It is away from a successful win relationship!

Uswitch And The 'Cash Saving Expert' Site

Cash Saving Expert was established by Martin Lewis, is situated in the UK, and flaunts one of the most moving affiliate marketing cases. The reason for this site is to show you how to set aside cash and teach you on principle money related instruments.

The topic of Money Saving Expert doesn't help utilize the affiliate frameworks of Amazon, eBay, or other necessary projects. In any case, this site is exceptionally productive gratitude to the affiliate connections of uSwitch, TotallyMoney, Tradedoubler, or Affiliate Window, among others. No ifs, ands or buts, one of those instances of affiliate marketing to mimic.

The Home Depot And The 'Buyer Search' Site

Buyer Search is your product suggestion and examination site. It was made in 1999 with an inquisitive crucial: take out the business distortion and deceptive nature of brands on the Internet.

By personally inspecting each new product, Consumer Search can suggest the most elite from every class and market niche. Because of the autonomy of its experts, the general population depends on the straightforwardness of its assessments.

Shopper Search income originates from connections to affiliates of The Home Depot, an incredible U.S. retailer of DIY and family unit products. While Consumer Search wins a commission for every deal, The Home Depot builds guest traffic and accomplishes ground-breaking backlinks.

eBay And The 'Wonder Cycles' Site

Wonder Cycles is the aftereffect of an astounding mix of BigCommerce and the eBay index. This online shop spends significant time in products and extras for cyclists, just as bikes and related hardware. As indicated by its makers, the strategic Glory Cycles is "to utilize the web to associate our clients with precisely what they are.

Wonder Cycles has been an extraordinary accomplishment since its dispatch in 2001, which isn't just because of the excellent administration of its originators. eBay and its supply of products have likewise contributed. Both have helped each other to make progress, which is one of the mainstays of affiliate marketing.

What Are The Best Affiliate Programs For Ecommerce?

As indicated by Business Insider, pay from the utilization of affiliate programs has developed by 10% per year since 2015, and this dynamic is relied upon to proceed until 2021. This marketing procedure is compelling for both online businesses and their partners.

Notwithstanding Amazon Associates and its notable affiliate program, numerous internet business organizations have comparative procedures. They stick out:

• Etsy Affiliates: Despite its low bonus of 4%, Etsy has one of the most intriguing affiliate programs, with a wide assortment of products that draw in a broad audience.

• eBay Affiliates: With exceptionally high commissions, somewhere in the range of 40% and 80%, eBay's affiliate program rivals Amazon's, offering different answers to adapt outsider websites and applications.

• The Zalando Partner Program: Zalando's affiliate payments are 8%. However, it has a wide choice of attire, frill, and shoes online to give. Like eBay, Amazon, or Etsy, Zalando has a client network and a perceived brand, which brings included worth.

• AliExpress Affiliate: with a variable commission of up to half, AliExpress rivals the past ones, and regardless of its short direction (it was propelled in 2010), its affiliate program is a reference in online business.

These and different instances of affiliate marketing are motivating. In any case, new businesses and moderate size organizations ought not to imagine that this marketing methodology is out of their span. Despite their size, division, or product, every single online retailer will prevail with regards to propelling their affiliate program.

Affiliate Marketing – Practical Examples Helps To Grow Brands

Prepared to get your image out there and tap into sections of your audience that you experience experienced issues coming to previously? If your answer is correct, at that point, affiliate marketing is actually what you should be paying regard for.

The reason is apparent. You associate with affiliates who will advance your image as an end-result of remuneration dependent on performance. As a trader, you possibly pay when the member can create brings about the type of lead age or deals. It couldn't be less complicated.

Then again, making sense of where to begin can be a test.

There are numerous roads that affiliates can use to advance your image. The way you decide to take is entirely needy upon your objectives and what your proposed advertising is going to best react to. Given this, we've assembled a couple of instances of affiliate marketing techniques with the goal that you can more readily survey, which will make the best fit for your image and your objectives.

Know Your Niche

You will have more noteworthy accomplishments with affiliate marketing if you put a little idea into who will be seeing your image. Without a doubt, some affiliate marketers are uncontrollably effective, advancing the scope of products and administrations. With the correct group, this can work.

In any case, the objective is to put your image is perspective on purchasers who are going to click and convert. For some brands, this implies concentrating on your niche advertising. The site howtocleananything.com is a curious case of niche-based affiliate marketing.

This site offers exhortation filled substance on the best way to clean everything. Honestly, from your Birkenstock ties to your gut button, they have it secured. While the guidance ranges from clinical consideration to family tips and everything in the middle of, it's wholly brought together under a typical topic. Each post contains and an affiliate connection, and guess what?

It bodes well when matched with the substance delivered to go with it.

This is an extraordinary case of how matching with the correct affiliate for your objective market can approach substantial gains in changes and your ROI.

Assemble Reviews... Lots of Them!

It doesn't make a difference what your image is, or how you're marketing it, audits matter. From a buyer point of view, they regularly affect picking your picture or your competitor's. More individuals trust surveys that they find online over those from a confided in companion or relative.

Primary concern? What buyers read about your product or administration online issue. One approach to utilize affiliate marketing is to pick affiliates that utilization an audit stage as the base of their site. One of our preferred models is NerdWallet.

Intended to administer down to earth counsel on everything monetary, NerdWallet offers surveys on a wide range of products and administrations identified with the budgetary business.

What truly affects with survey-based affiliates is decency. Search for branches that produce top quality, edible substance. You need a certified vibe from your members when they're looking into your image.

It's an extraordinary thought to manufacture a relationship with your affiliates before starting work together. Think about the contribution of your product or administration to the affiliate for gratis for them to utilize and get to know before they start advancing your product. A brand that has personal experiences is going to put on a show of being sincere to your target group.

Affiliates That Offer Real-World Value

There are two things that individuals are hoping to escape the substance they see on the web. They either need to be engaged; they need the material to include a massive incentive in their life or both. If you are adjusting yourself to an affiliate, which depends on content creation, ensure that what they are delivering meets the criteria for progress. Probably the best substance for affiliate marketing offers a whole world, down to earth appeal that will keep the audience returning for additional. We should take a gander at MoneySavingExpert, for instance.

At the point when you land here, the primary thing you notice is that the site is stuffed with content. To start with, it's all quality substance that is exceptionally applicable to the intended interest group. Also, there's something irregular about this site. It gets no cash from publicists. All income originates from affiliate joins.

Stop and consider that for a moment. Affiliate joins are performance-based. That implies this site possibly brings in cash when those connections produce activity. Do you figure they would continue utilizing this model if it wasn't working for them? We're speculating the response to that question is no, so they should make a significant activity for their affiliate vendors.

Coupon Sites, Deals and Promotions

Another method for extending your image's scope through affiliate marketing is by having a nearness on destinations that are set up to offer coupons, arrangements, and advancements on accomplice brands explicitly. While this sort of affiliate relationship unexpectedly works apiece, however, with the correct procedure, it very well may be similarly viable. For instance, Nomad Coffee Club uses this well by joining forces with bloggers doing giveaways and product audits alongside particular limits.

Instead of utilizing substance and impact to push your image, you depend on the purchaser's affection for a deal. Any individual who looks around online realizes that finding the best arrangement is a piece of good times. Coupon locales assist them with an excursion by interfacing them with the best method on your product or administration.

You support a coupon or advancement. The site posts it, alongside those of different brands that they are working with. The way to making this work is understanding that your SEO technique should be upgraded to create results for you on their page. A large number of the best arrangement destinations will help with this procedure.

Pause, Did We Forget to Mention Video? To what extent has it taken you to peruse this article as yet? 5 minutes possibly? Something astounding has occurred in that measure of time.

Around 1,500 hours of YouTube content has been transferred. Consistently, there are 300 hours of video assigned for review. Presently, consider what it could mean for your image if you had a nearness on a portion of that video content. The potential is gigantic.

Affiliates with a YouTube nearness can advance your image legitimately, or through a pennant on their video. Exactly how effective can YouTube affiliate marketing be? Simply see this person.

Ou may know him as the friendly face behind Ryan's Toy Review, or you may know him as the $11 million affiliate master. The reason for this affiliate marketing procedure is that a YouTube influencer/superstar advances your product or administration in their video, right now audits. The drawback is that it very well may be increasingly hard to follow traffic with this kind of relationship, except if a connection is incorporated with the substance.

The upside is that the video is immense. It's the favored sort of substance for most web clients, particularly those that are getting to content from their cell phones. This implies your image gets put before a more prominent, increasingly drew in audience, which involves more transformations and benefits in your pocket.

That is a Start, But What Else?

Along these lines, there were some extraordinary instances of various styles if affiliate marketing. It takes more than guides to begin, and you additionally need some useful exhortation. Here are five hints to remember, regardless of what kind of affiliate marketing you decide for your image.

1. A little research implies cash in your pocket. Before you begin, you have to have a thought of what your rivals are doing and what they're paying to get it going. To draw in the best affiliates, your rates should be severe.

2. Speaking of rates, it's satisfactory to have a couple of stunts at your disposal. Consider having a level rate that you offer to all affiliates, including every single new agreement. At that point, have a second remuneration level for your best-performing affiliate accomplices.

3. Start on the correct foot. Openness is of the utmost importance. If you can't impart promptly and effectively with your affiliates, at that point, it's presumably not going to be the best working relationship for you. You need to have the option to share product subtleties, deal data, rules, and even conceptualize how your image could be best advanced.

4. Have a lot of rules set up. Choose how much freedom your affiliates can take with your image. It is correct to say that you are okay with them offering a rebate that you didn't affirm or utilizing your product such that it wasn't expected? Put forward all the guidelines before you begin.

5. Have a financial limit at the top of the priority list, yet be versatile. If you've arrived at where you've met or surpassed your affiliate marketing spending plan, see what it's accomplished for you regarding ROI. In case you're creating deals and a decent benefit, there's no motivation to adhere to the specific numbers you've written down.

CHAPTER NINE

EARNING WITH AFFILIATE MARKETING

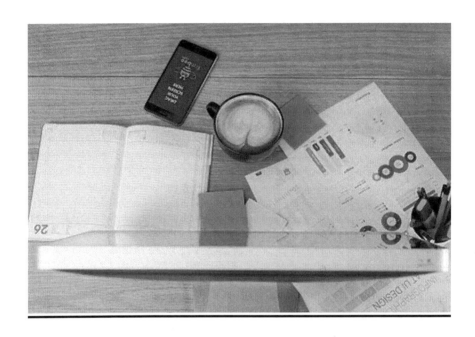

Could You Make Money With Affiliate Marketing?

Would you be able to bring in cash with affiliate marketing? The short answer is true; affiliate projects can procure additional money and even full-time pay from home. The long answer is somewhat more confounded. Like any home pay adventure, achievement comes less from what you decide to do to bring in cash, yet whether you do what should be done effectively and reliably.

The Reality of Affiliate Marketing

The issue with affiliate marketing, in the same way as other self-start venture alternatives, are the supposed masters and make accessible money programs that propose affiliate marketing should be possible quickly and with little exertion. Chances are you've perused cases of affiliate marketing programs that state you can make countless dollars a month doing nothing. Or on the other hand, they recommend you can set up your affiliate site, and afterward overlook it, but to check your bank stores.

The truth in affiliate marketing is that it resembles most other work-at-home endeavors; there are rare sorts of incredibly wealthy people, a significant number who are sufficient enough to meet their objectives, and a ton who aren't making anything.

The inquiry isn't generally whether affiliate marketing is a practical salary choice (it is); however, whether you can make affiliate marketing work for you. No one but you can conclude that, however, to enable you to complete, you can check our past post on the advantages and disadvantages of Affiliate Marketing.

To what extent did It Take Other Affiliate Marketers before They Started Making Money?

While the facts confirm that "it depends," I will expect that you're savvy enough to realize that. It relies upon your niche, how long you put in per week, how genuine you are tied in with succeeding, and how quick (or moderate) of a student you are. Hell, even karma assumes a job.

Be that as it may, you know the entirety of this. You simply need a general answer. Would you be able to begin bringing in cash this week? This month? This year? With affiliate marketing, to what extent does it take?

Here's the exact reply answer, and you probably won't care for it. Affiliate marketing takes around a year to begin seeing achievement. In any event, a visible and reliable achievement that is the thing that most expert Affiliate Marketers said.

I can hear you now... "A YEAR?! That is to say, I need to invested energy, cash, and exertion for a YEAR before I see any achievement?"

Practically, in any case, I accept with shockingly better arranging, vision, objective, and challenging work, you can begin procuring cold cash in 6 Months!

Presently, this doesn't mean you won't bring in cash when you simply start; this solitary implies that your income will be capricious, sparse, and conflicting.

The amount Can You Earn from Affiliate Marketing?

Two inquiries we regularly get posed:

"What amount is it conceivable to win from affiliate marketing?"

"If I quit my place of employment, to what extent will it take me to acquire X/day?"

The two answers rely upon your fitness, yet I understand there are an unquenchable want reliable figures. In this way, here's my interpretation of the issue...

There are five gaining sections right now.

Affiliate Apprentice – Losing cash.

Low-Level Affiliate – Anywhere from 0N - N5,000

Halfway Affiliate – Anywhere from N5,000/day up to N50,000/day.

Significant Level Affiliate – Anything above N50,000/day.

One of the different laws of Affiliate Marketing is: "Income is vanity and benefit is Sanity."

As it were, if a person is making an income of N100,000 per day and a benefit of N5,000 and someone else wins N50,000 in revenue; however, a profit of N10,000. The subsequent person is in an ideal situation when contrasted with the primary affiliate marketer.

Adjusting Expectations to Earning Potential

My response to the inquiry, "If I quit my place of employment, to what extent will it take me to gain X/day?" is regularly a quick "Perpetually," and here's the reason.

Numerous affiliates neglect to adjust their procuring desires to work that is really equipped for conveying the ideal salary.

Here's a breakdown of where each kind of affiliate is probably going to contribute his time:

Low-Level Affiliates: Focuses on pockets of benefit around the web. He overlooks economies of scale for high edge battles on littler traffic sources that will, in general, be incredibly unstable.

Models incorporate dating destinations, little scope Facebook Ads, Juicy Ad purchases.

Middle Affiliates: Focuses on high volume traffic sources with littler edges than the Beginner, however more volume. They are indecently grouped around the dating niche (and all the more as of late grown-up dating). Intense rivalry on massive traffic sources lessens the size of the pie for all—keen movers right now versatile marketing and pop traffic.

Significant Level Affiliates: Focuses on mass-advertise media purchases and enormously versatile traffic sources. Regularly exchanges comfort (self-serve traffic hotspots) for direct investments with better edges and the entirety of the pie. More serious hazards included, progressively capital required.

How Speedily Can One Make Money With Affiliate Marketing?

Individuals new to this entire web marketing business come in not just hoping to bring in cash online as though it was an undeniable right to web clients, yet they additionally need to make it quick!

In any case, how quick would you be able to bring in cash with affiliate marketing?

This is an inquiry I get day by day either on the Wealthy Affiliate stage, where I tutor my understudies or through the inbox.

While I do comprehend the inquiry and the significance behind it, it's tough to offer a straight and proper response to it.

If you simply need to bring in cash quick with affiliate marketing, at that point, I am unfortunately this business isn't for you.

I don't know about some other business (on the web or disconnected) that can bring in cash as quickly as some would anticipate that it should be (if you are aware of something if it's not too much trouble, let me know in the remark area underneath).

Additionally, I don't get your meaning by quick?

Do you mean a day, a week, or a month?

There are various degrees of "quick" here, and keeping in mind that I do trust it's conceivable to begin bringing in cash rather rapidly, you're in all probability must do in any event 6 to a year of work before you start seeing some outcome worth gloating about.

Presently, when I offer that response to whoever asks, generally, I don't recover an answer, yet in some cases, I do get the infrequent "Why?".

I wouldn't fret noting this. I am here to assist individuals with beginning with affiliate marketing, so if they need to realize to what extent it will take them and why it would take such a long time, I am glad to reply.

Here's the reason it will take you a couple of months up to an entire year before you begin seeing a few outcomes.

The 'Affiliate Marketing" Learning Curve

If you are a prepared affiliate marketer with experience in building beneficial niche destinations, (above all else you wouldn't ask) yet, also, you do get an opportunity of bringing in cash in the initial barely any weeks or somewhere in the vicinity.

The explanation for this is there is an expectation to absorb information that you necessarily need to get over on your approach to making full-time wealth with affiliate marketing.

Simply think about the advantages of affiliate marketing for a second:

1. Free time

2. Be your chief

3. You find a good pace while you rest

4. and so forward.

You think these advantages are going to simply fall on your lap since you chose to google "how to bring in cash with affiliate marketing?".

Indeed, even with all the assets on the planet to show you (and I will give you my best preparing underneath), you, despite everything, are going to need to gain proficiency with the procedure – and it is anything but a process you can adapt rapidly.

There are a ton of things that you have to know before you begin bringing in any cash and that that incorporates figuring out how to develop a website, understanding watchword research and how it applies to affiliate marketing, composing content, fixing your substance, discover niche affiliate projects to join, etc.

Simply that would take you, in any event, a month to truly nail it down "like a master," and that is just if you are placing in at any rate 6 to 8 hours of work each day.

Presently I am sure that a great deal of you don't have that sort of additional time on your hands that you can simply commit to watching video aides and pursuing affiliate programs.

The point being is that regardless of whether you do things directly as it so happens, which is hard yet possible with the correct preparation, you are taking a gander in any event 2 to 3 months to begin seeing some salary and learning all the ropes.

You Need To Build The Traffic First

One thing individuals who need to bring in cash quick with affiliate marketing disregard is the way that you need an audience to offer to.

Building an audience sufficiently large to bring in cash from and developing it to believe you likewise require significant investment.

Presently once more, you can do this in a month, or you can do this in a year; everything relies upon a lot of factors; however, in any case, it will set aside an effort to get an ace.

There are affiliate marketing niches that will, in general, bring in cash quicker than others; however, you indeed must be fortunate to discover something you need to advance, that pays well, and there's practically no opposition in.

How Quickly Can You Start Making Money With Affiliate Marketing?

You can begin from today, yes, today.

As the old Chinese saying goes, the best time to plant a tree was 20 years prior; the subsequent best time is today.

If you are prepared to acknowledge the way that you won't make "quick cash" with affiliate marketing, at that point the open door is directly here before you to begin learning and working to ideally in a couple of months have the option to make steady pay with your new side-hustle.

Presently I cannot guarantee you that you will be effective. However, I can assure you – an even better assurance that if you read the rest of this post, you will be destined for success in bringing some respectable cash in the coming a very long time with affiliate marketing.

To what extent will It Take to Make Money with Affiliate Marketing?

Utilizing the above strategies, mainly if you follow the Wealthy Affiliate guide, you will undoubtedly have seen some achievement in as little as 2 to 3 months, with a full-opportunity pay coming in anyplace between month 7 and 12.

You may believe it's far to go the time yet will pass in any case.

You can spend it either looking into data bouncing from one blog entry to the next, or you can begin from today and know precisely where you will be in a couple of months.

"What amount is it conceivable to acquire from affiliate marketing?" "If I quit my place of employment, to what extent will it take me to win X/day?"

The two answers rely upon your fitness. However, I understand there's an unquenchable yearning for reliable figures. Along these lines, here's my interpretation of the issue...

There are five procuring sections right now.

1. Affiliate Apprentice – Losing cash.

2. Low-Level Affiliate – Anywhere from $0/day up to $300/day.

3. Intermediate Affiliate – Anywhere from $300/day up to $3,000/day.

4. High-Level Affiliate – Anything above $3,000/day.

5. The 'Pack of Dicks' Affiliate – He who considers anything short of $10,000/day to be 'treating it terribly.'

We were exposed at the top of the priority list that we're discussing benefit here, not income.

Technically, a person procuring $300,000/month in income could be more awful off than the person making a consistent $100/day with no outgoings. He would need to be visually impaired, imbecilic, hard of hearing, alcoholic, and idiotic to keep gulping such a thin edge. Yet, it features one of the different laws of affiliate marketing:

Income is vanity, and the benefit is mental stability.

A remarkable trait of our industry is how the powerful can fall medium-term, regularly in great design.

You can go from acquiring $3,000/day to grass all in about a midday break, what's more, the other way around.

An Intermediate affiliate may drop a level after losing his best battle. At the same time, the Affiliate Apprentice can turn Top Doggy Baller medium-term if he lurches into an unsaturated niche and makes it pay (a day by day event in 2009, uncommon in 2013).

The Bag of Dicks Affiliate may keep on prospering, or lack of concern may chomp him in the arse. However, he'll generally be a sack of dicks as long as he makes a decision about others for how cheerful they ought to be with their pay.

$300/Day versus $300/Today

Numerous affiliates can't tell their day by day salary from their present pay.

The unstable idea of the business makes it a thoughtless dream to compute your yearly compensation on the rear of one day's benefits.

If this is your first day of affiliate marketing and you gain $1000, don't expect that you'll bank $365,000 in the following year.

Your present profit, comparable to compensation, is $2.73/day.

Rehash your prosperity tomorrow, at that point the following day, etc. into the not so distant when you be able to begin tossing out unconventional multipliers on a salary that isn't yet yours.

What Are Established Affiliates Earning?

In the setup affiliate network, I would state that the majority of us operate in the Intermediate procuring class.

Note that by 'set up,' I'm discussing affiliates working all day in the CPA space.

Just as of late, a survey was hung on the STM Forum (I prescribe you join) asking, "What amount do you acquire in a year?"

That is a ton of moolah in anyone's money.

If you take the middle of this little example ($81,000 to $120,000), it means between $221/day and $328/day in benefit. I would put this at the very beginning of the Intermediate section, mostly because the salary must be continued throughout a year. What's more, this section is the place most settled affiliates remain.

Note: Not all affiliate discussions are made equivalent. If you somehow happened to take a middle example from The Warrior Forum, I'd wager my crap that the average profit would scarcely cover the run of the mill London gas bill.

The bounce from winning $300/day to acquiring $3,000/day and continuing it is the thing that isolates a fruitful, built up CPA affiliate from the absolute best in the business.

It's significant, the best in the business are not generally the most joyful with their salaries.

Adjusting Expectations to Earning Potential

My response to the inquiry, "If I quit my place of employment, to what extent will it take me to win X/day?" is regularly a quick "Always," and here's the reason.

Numerous affiliates neglect to adjust their acquiring desires to work that is equipped for conveying the ideal salary.

Here's a breakdown of where each sort of affiliate is probably going to contribute his time:

Low-Level Affiliates: Focuses on pockets of benefit around the web. He disregards economies of scale for high edge crusades on littler traffic sources that will, in general, be incredibly unstable. Models incorporate POF dating efforts, little scope Facebook Ads, Juicy Ad purchases.

Middle of the road Affiliates: Focuses on high volume traffic sources with littler edges than the Beginner, yet more volume. Disgustingly grouped around the dating niche (and all the more as of late grown-up dating). Intense rivalry on enormous traffic sources lessens the size of the pie for all—brilliant movers right now portable marketing and pop traffic.

Elevated Level Affiliates: Focuses on mass market media purchases and colossally adaptable traffic sources. Frequently exchanges accommodation (self-serve traffic hotspots) for direct purchases with better edges and the entirety of the pie. More serious hazards included, progressively capital required.

Understudy Affiliates – Focuses, perpetually, on the entirety of the above mentioned, to his burden.

Sack of Dicks Affiliate – Focuses on Fox News.

Things being what they are, what would you like to be? What are you glad to be?

If your desires are to such an extent that you are pleased with an extra $100/day, at that point screw anyone who instructs you to toss down $10,000 on an expensive media purchase, POF is a splendid low-level traffic source (with a couple of Intermediate individual cases which depend on economies of extension), and you need never change your jacket.

If you are content with the middle of the road winning section, at that point in like manner, you can stand to maintain a strategic distance from direct purchases and hazardous speculations; however, you will most likely need to progress past the okay pockets of benefit supported by beginners.

Notwithstanding, if you are the sort of affiliate who's going to feel like he lets loose missing until he's gaining $5,000/day, at that point, take a rude awakening.

Is it accurate to say that you are submitting your time and vitality to the kinds of battles that are measurably and strategically prone to open up the acquiring potential that speaks to what you need?

There's no reason for cutting out small scale niches on POF if your heart thumps for a million-dollar pay.

It's an essential procedure.

What are you going to chip away at that can convey a salary that you're content with?

Fuck, that is an instruction forever, not merely affiliate marketing.

We CPA affiliates will go in general float towards High-Level pay targets, most likely because we are youthful, voracious, offensive, unshowered mountain trolls with a hunger forever's extravagances.

Furthermore, that is fine. However, there's a trick.

Everyone has an acquiring edge that speaks to a state of unavoidable losses—furthermore, many neglect to remember it.

Your life circumstance may direct that $200/day is the apex of money related inspiration. You can drive yourself to achieve this objective, yet any further and the motivation starts to slip. That is a state of consistent losses. Consider it your usual range of familiarity. Any work to progress past this point accompanies the extra weight of pushing you out of that safe place, and thus delaying sets in, alongside the double devastating feelings of trepidation of disappointment and achievement.

Numerous affiliates battle to take their businesses to the following level because the idea of the game is to such an extent that you can be a 'Halfway' banking one of the top 1% of pay rates in the populace.

Why drive it further?

There's a valid justification why we must be forceful, greedier, and pushier than most. Affiliate marketing isn't a lifelong stepping stool in any conventional sense.

We are just ever as effective as our last crusades.

We can't advance through the positions. There aren't any. There are no fallbacks, no safe arrivals, and no space for a performance marketer to live off past wonders.

CONCLUSION

Affiliate marketing isn't hard, yet it requires information, arranging, and reliable exertion to make any critical pay. Your general odds of bringing in cash with an affiliate program are most likely no preferable and no more terrible over some other kind of web-based business. Your financial progress relies upon how well you execute your affiliate business plan.

While there isn't a great deal of cost in firing up as an affiliate marketer, there are a couple of things that you have to do if you genuinely need to bring in cash marketing others' products. One of the essential requirements for any effective affiliate program is to have your very own site. While it is conceivable to buy promotion space on locales and to publicize through Google Adwords, this is a momentary technique setting up an essential website that has a specific center that will have a significant effect on the accomplishment of your program. Remember that your site doesn't need to be confounded with a ton of blaze media, liveliness, or other extravagant fancy odds and ends. If you plan on concentrating on affiliate marketing systems that focus on the home purchaser, you are in an ideal situation with a first site that will stack rapidly on a dial-up association. Dial-up is still amazingly famous in various areas.

Online payments are an incredible method to get your affiliate payments and monitor your profit effectively. From this holy messenger, you might need to investigate opening a record with one of the more famous online administrations that send and get reserves. E.g., PayPal. Another significant perspective is deciding exactly what your contact data will be, in regards to correspondence with your affiliate program. This would incorporate an email Address and physical postage information. The email address ought to be one you have put aside explicitly for your marketing business.

Picking the best products for your specific circumstance have to do with what you know and the amount you think about it. For instance, a person that has worked in media communications for several years will most likely see a lot about communication, related administrations, and innovation that are utilized inside that industry. Another angle about setting up with the correct products to elevate has to do with where you see a niche to fill in. Finding a populace or business division that gives off an impression of being, to a great extent, overlooked in the marketing procedure can give the motivation you have to make a fruitful affiliate marketing program.

Try not to permit yourself to get debilitated just because everything isn't apparent as you start this piece of the procedure. Rehearsing some persistence and allowing yourself to locate the correct products to advance as a component of the program will just serve to make you progressively devoted to the accomplishment of the program. At last, you will discover the products that will prompt an extremely useful affiliate marketing plan and give you an attractive income stream, yet additionally a great deal of personal fulfillment.

Made in the USA
Columbia, SC
19 July 2020